Love God?

BRONWEN SCOTT-BRANAGAN

National Library of Australia Cataloguing-in-Publication entry

Creator: Scott-Branagan, Bronwen, author.

Title: Do you love god? / Bronwen Scott-Branagan.

ISBN: 9780992599645 (paperback)

Notes: Includes bibliographical references.

Subjects: God (Christianity)--Worship and love.
God--Worship and love--Biblical teaching.
Trinity--Biblical teaching.

Dewey Number: 204.3

TABLE OF CONTENTS

'And one of the scribes...asked him, "Which commandment is the most important of all?"

Jesus answered,

"The most important is,...

'Hear O Israel, the Lord our God, the Lord is one. And you shall love the Lord your God with all your heart and with all your soul and with all your mind and with all your strength.'

The second is this: 'You shall love your neighbour as yourself.'

There is no other commandment greater than these."

Mark 12.28 – 31(ESV)

CHAPTER ONE

THE QUESTION

It was nearly midnight, or felt like it. Too weary to negotiate the car into the garage, I parked it outside in the street. Bible Study at the Home Group I attend seemed to have gone on forever that night and I was glad to be home.

As I pressed my car's remote lock, the door of a car on the opposite side of the street slammed shut. I turned to see in the dim beams of the streetlight a neighbour walking towards me.

"Can I ask you something?"

"Yes, of course."

"Do you love God?"

This question was followed by a momentary pause as I shot up an arrow prayer: '*Help, Lord, I am not worthy to answer, but I do love you. Even if doubts come I know you are; that you were Love before the world began and if ever I have any doubts the problem is within myself. I know I only need to ask and your Holy Spirit will teach me how to respond. Please help me right now*!'

So I continued,

"Yes, I do."

Obviously such a question required a broader response than that. She was an intelligent woman and must have asked because it was something she had been thinking about. Possibly she did not want to know about my relationship with God, but was thinking of her own. A much more comprehensive reply was needed. What could I say?

"I love Him very much. The first thing I think of is the Ten Commandments that God gave to Moses so long ago on Mount Sinai and the way that centuries later Jesus summed them up so succinctly:

> *'You shall love the Lord your God with all your heart... and your neighbour as yourself.'* [1]

"Look, it's late. In the morning I'll think of a better answer and I'll come over and see you. I'll look on my bookshelves, too, and try and find a book with something more about it that might be helpful. See you tomorrow."

Once inside my home, I spent some time scanning the contents of my bookshelves, but could not find anything that seemed to be really suitable; it would have to wait until morning. The next day I went to my computer and searched online, but could not find what I had envisaged there either. Finally I contacted my local Christian bookshop.

The only book that the lass who answered my telephone call could recommend was *'The Four Loves'* by a Christian academic, who had been a lecturer at both Oxford and Cambridge Universities, and friend of Tolkien, C. S. Lewis. The book was ordered and I called over to tell my friend that we might have to wait a few days. When *'The Four Loves'* arrived a few days later, I flipped through it fairly quickly. At first I thought it wasn't really what I had hoped for. Nevertheless, it seemed to be all that was available, so I lent it to my friend. After reading it, she returned it, saying,

---

[1] Matthew 22. 37 – 39 (ESV)

"It really wasn't what I was looking for. "

On reading further and digging deeper I found that it had so much that was, in a way, hidden, and, being the work of C. S. Lewis, of course there is some real treasure there. However, it was written some years ago now, and the language was, perhaps, a little dated. It was important that I really answered this question. After all, loving God is at the heart of our Christian faith, so I decided to do some research and write it down for her, but with the hope that it may encourage someone else, too.

Do you love God?

This query has given me the opportunity to look at a crucial question about our Christian faith from several different points of view, for me to learn more as I do and to share it with others. This question appears to be simple, and the reply can be quite straightforward as well, either we do love God or we don't, but a simple answer does not begin to cover all the aspects. If we look into it more deeply we need to try to find the underlying basis of the formation of our notions or beliefs.

After some thought, prayer and reading of the Scriptures, it seemed that a response to this question can be made up of many different facets, just like the different faces on a diamond or precious stone like those my husband used to spend hours cutting when it was one of his hobbies. The cutting and the shaping of the stone, and of our understanding of our faith, is important. Within the facets, of both stone and question, is where we find the spark and the fire. This can lead us to view the question from different angles to find the answer we seek:

- We can look at the question from a linguistic point of view
- We can unpack the question to reveal each separate nugget (and they are nuggets, as each word can reveal so much treasure)
- We can examine the question from a philosophical viewpoint

If we analyze this question from different angles, including linguistically and philosophically, it may seem a little artificial at first, but also it can help to solve our dilemma. On the other hand, these angles may seem to be rather objective and impersonal; it begins to become clear that it demands of us as well that we examine it from a personal point of view. By doing this this we can hope to find how, as we delve deeper, we can go right to the crux of the matter, the basics of our Christian beliefs. These in turn involve our own hearts and feelings; as Christians, we know that God loves us - the Bible tells us so:

> *'But now thus says the Lord, ... because you are precious in my eyes... I love you.*[2]
>
> When we open our eyes to truly look, we discover that we can see His love and care surrounding us in many ways. So how *can* we solve this perplexing issue and love God in the way that we feel we should?

Remember that lovely promise Jesus made:

> *'Ask, and it will be given to you; seek, and you will find; knock, and it will be opened to you, For everyone who asks receives, and the one who seeks finds, and to the one who knocks it will be opened...If*

---

[2] Isaiah 43.1, 4 (ESV)

you then, who are evil, know how to give good gifts to your children, how much more will your Father who is in heaven give good things to those who ask him!'[3]

DISCUSSION

1. Do you ever use 'arrow' prayers?
2. Have you ever wondered if God is too busy to answer your prayers?
3. Does God always answer our prayers immediately? Why do you think that is so?
4. Do you think that the imagery of the facet is helpful or intrusive?
5. Do you truly feel that God loves you?

Prayer

Loving Father God, Creator of the whole universe and of me, open my eyes to a greater understanding of the Scriptures and open my heart to your love. May I see with clarity of vision all you have done for me in the past, even when I have had my mind and heart closed to you. Help me to learn more of your great love for all your children and for me, so that my love for you may grow more and more. I ask this in the name of Jesus. Amen.

[3] Matthew 7. 7 – 11 (ESV)

NOTES

CHAPTER TWO

A LINGUISTIC POINT OF VIEW - 1

Do you love God?

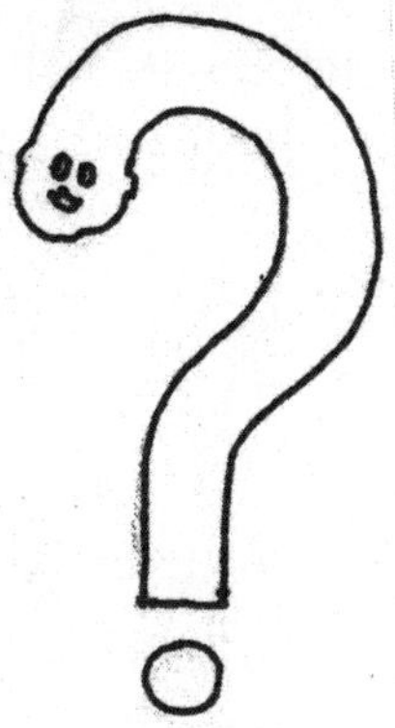

Firstly, let me apologize for looking at this question from a linguistics point of view. Having been trained and having lectured in the field of Applied Linguistics, for me it is the logical place to begin, but I admit that to others it may seem strange. Language is what most humans use to communicate.

Those who study the science of linguistics, including those seemingly few stalwarts who teach grammar these days, tell us that this type of question is known as a 'closed question.' It only requires a Yes/No answer. But this particular query was asked in all seriousness and obviously requires a serious and more comprehensive reply. A response of 'Yes,' or 'No,' will not do at all.

If we want to gain more knowledge on a linguistic topic, we may find that we really need to think about asking the question in a different way.

How can we do that?

We could ask our question using what are known as the '*wh*' questions, even though they do not all begin with those two letters: *why, when, which, what, where* and this list of words also includes *how*. By beginning our question with one of these words, we may help to provide a broader response, and that is just what we require. We asked our question because we really wanted to know the answer.

By the use of the '*wh*' words, we can ask the question in six different ways. These should help to clarify for us what we really want to know. Let us look at how we could use each of these '*wh*' questions and perhaps they can help in our search by extending the ideas that they engender.

a. **WHY**: Why do we love God? Why does He love us? Why should we share that love?

   Why do we love God?
   St. John, as well as being the probable author of what we call the fourth Gospel, also wrote some letters that are included further on in the New Testament. Near the end of the first of these letters,[4] he wrote:
   '*We love Him because He first loved us.*'

   We are told in Genesis, the very first book of the Bible that our Father God, our great Creator formed us in His own image.[5] We were made quite differently from all the rest of God's creation: we were given a great ability to think, to communicate with each other and with God, to know the difference between what is right and what is wrong, to laugh, which no other creature can do, and to create. We need to remember that all this beneficence from our Heavenly Father does not make us gods; our Creator reigns supreme. *God is love*;[6] we were created to love:

[4] 1 John 4.19 (KJV)
[5] Genesis 1. 26, 27
[6] 1 John 4.16 (KJV)

'According as he has chosen us in him before the foundation of the world, that we should be holy and without blame before him in love'.[7]

Why does He love us?
God loves us because He created us, but He also gave us the power of choice[8] and He loves all those who choose to call themselves His children. He gave His Son, Jesus Christ, as a sacrifice on the cross so that our sins could be forgiven. When we accept this amazing gift, through Jesus' sacrifice our sins can be forgiven and God can make us holy.

'If we confess our sins, he is faithful and just to forgive us our sins, and to cleanse us from all unrighteousness.'[9]

That is what that word 'righteousness' is all about: when we ask for forgiveness through Jesus our sins are forgiven and we are made right with God. Then we are made holy so that we can come close to our Father God who is so holy and have fellowship with Him.

Why should we share that love?
Communication with each other is vital. It helps us to build up our friendships, so we come into fellowship with each other; that fellowship should be the reason why we share God's love. He loves us but we can't keep that bounty, that gracious gift of

---

[7] Ephesians 1. 4 (KJV)
[8] *See* Deuteronomy 30.15-20 (KJV)
[9] 1 John 1.9 (KJV)

His love, to ourselves. It is too great, too wonderful! Jesus' final summing up of the Ten Commandments, what is sometimes called the Royal Command,[10] ends with telling us that we should love our neighbours as ourselves. If we love our neighbours and are concerned for their spiritual welfare, then we must share God's love with them.

This is important; St. John's first Letter that has been preserved in the New Testament points out that if we say, *"I love God"* but hate our brother, then we are liars. This is a major warning. John uncompromisingly concludes that Jesus' Commandment to love our neighbour logically includes the deduction that *'whoever loves God must also love his brother.'*[11] To say that we love God and then just keep that great news to ourselves means that we don't really love Him at all, it's just so much meaningless hot air.

The words 'neighbours' and 'brothers' (and sisters) infers that we should share God's love with anyone who needs our love and help, whether in our homes, our neighbourhood or around the world.

b. **WHEN:** When should we love God? When should we tell God that we love Him?

When should we love God?

We should love God always and at all times. He shows us in so many ways every day in our lives that He loves and cares for us – and will love us

---

[10] *See* p. 4

[11] 1 John 4.20 – 21 (ESV)

always and forever. With a love like that we can love Him for eternity. Do you remember that well-known verse, John 3. 16 (KJV):

> *'For God so loved the world that he gave his only begotten Son, that whosoever believeth in him should not perish, but have everlasting life.'*

When we believe and trust in Jesus, we will have joy in the loving presence of God forever.

When should we tell God that we love Him?

Anytime. All the time. When we talk to Him in our prayers, when we worship and praise His great glory. We know that God is with us always, but we sometimes get involved in the many claims on our lives that keep us so busy that we forget about Him – and then something happens that causes us to come back. He hasn't gone away, but we have been so busy that we may have gone away and completely forgotten about Him.

I remember a story I heard in Children's Story time in church when I was quite young: during the English Civil War, which was in the middle of the 1600s, Jacob Astley, the first Baron Astley of Reading in England, prayed before battle:

> *"O Lord, Thou knowest how busy I must be this day. If I forget Thee, do not Thou forget me."*[12]

---

[12] http://en.wikipedia.org/wiki/Jacob_Astley,_1st_Baron_Astley_of_Reading

c. **WHICH:** Which god do we love? Which god should we choose to love?

Which god do we love?

A god is an object, a thing, or person of value and consequence to us that we put first in our lives; it can be anything that we allow to have power over us in our human lives. It becomes what we revere, honour and adore: *what* or *whom* we worship. That's just the way that God made us; it is part of our id: our basic, inherited instincts, needs and feelings.

There are many people, events and possessions that we can love and that we can put first in our lives and loves.

Should it be the person who is the love of my life?
Is it football, cricket, swimming, mountaineering or some other physical activity that comes first in my heart?
Could it possibly be my own status at the cat-fight-cat that happens so frequently as we strive to mount the corporate ladder at work?
Is it my position in the family or my beloved children?
Could it even be how I would like other people to view me at church? Should it be my possessions, my bank account?
Do I love myself better than anything else in life?

If I am being really honest, I must ask myself if this god really meets my deepest spiritual needs – and I must answer it truthfully.

Which god should we choose to love?
When Almighty God, our Heavenly Father, created us, He gave us free choice; but remember, it's the choice of a lifetime – and beyond! We are warned to be alert and aware; our selection affects the whole of our future, here - and in the hereafter. Don't treat this choice lightly!

This choice requires careful, prayerful thought; our lives here and in the hereafter depend on it.

d. **WHERE:** Where do we find God's love? Where do we love God?

Where do we find God's love?

We can find God's love for us in so many different places. It may be as we experience the beauty of the wonderful natural world that He created. It may be that we can find it in the peace of a gentle sea as it laps softly on the shore, as we lift our eyes to the mountains, see the glory of a sunset or find it in the trusting eyes of a little child.

It may be that we feel His love around us in an inexplicable way when we suddenly open the eyes of our hearts and allow ourselves to see it.

We can learn about God's love in the Bible; the Scriptures are God's message of His love all through history as it comes down to us, His people. We can see God's love in other people as they share that love with us, and we can see it especially in Christians who have invited God, the Holy Spirit, to live in their hearts.

Where do we find His love? It is all around us, surrounding us - if we look for it with our whole hearts and open our eyes to see it. Then we can celebrate it and share it with others.

Where do we love God?

God's all-embracing love may, of course, be found in churches, in beautiful, hallowed buildings that have been houses of prayer for many years, or we may find it in uplifting services complete with glorious music and choirs. We may come upon it unexpectedly when we suddenly see the beauty of His creation in the design of a tiny flower, the intricate pattern of a rather insignificant seashell, or in the glory of a brilliant sunset that illuminates, not just the whole world around us, but remains shining in our hearts as well. These places and times may be where we are most aware of God's love and so they can be where we lift up our hearts to Him, full to overflowing with our love and thanks.

Sometimes other Christians share the joy of special events and milestones in their Christian journey with us and other Christians. On such occasions we may suddenly discover God's love for us in their stories and then our hearts are especially warmed as we share in the joy of that heavenly love.

Window at St. George's Guesthouse, Jerusalem

DISCUSSION

1. Do you think that looking at God's love in these ways is helpful?
2. Have you learned John 3.16 by heart and understood the depth of this statement?
3. What other reasons might you have for loving God?
4. What other gods do you need to be aware of in case they become too important in your life?
5. Read the hymn, '*Sometimes a Light Surprises.*' Has this ever happened to you?
6. Where are your favourite places to find peace so you can enjoy the beauty of God's powerful presence in your life?

Prayer

Father God, help me when I need to make choices in this life to do it in obedience to your will for the direction and path that I should follow. Give me wisdom and strength to choose only You, Father, Son and Holy Spirit, and may I love You, Lord, with all my heart and mind. In the Name of Jesus. Amen.

NOTES

CHAPTER THREE

A LINGUISTIC POINT OF VIEW - 2

e. **HOW:** How do we love God? How can I show God's love?

How do we love God?
I know that I love God, I have learned about His love in the Scriptures and in life, but I wonder if that is enough. Is there some special way that I should love Him?

We can read in St. Matthew's Gospel about the time when a prominent lawyer asked Jesus which of the Commandments was the most important. Jesus replied:

> *'You shall love the Lord your God with all your heart and with all your soul and with all your mind.'* He added that *'This is the great and first commandment.'*[13]

Our liturgy, the set form that we use in church services, can become so familiar that we don't always really listen and understand the depth of meaning in those beautiful words. They are mostly taken directly from the Scriptures but in our liturgy we find that another word is added.

---

[13] Matthew 22.37 – 38 (ESV)

We can find that recorded in St. Mark's Gospel:

> *'...and with all your strength.'*[14]

When Jesus was travelling the countryside and cities with His message, Mark was just a young lad; we only meet him in the Gospel records near the end of Jesus' ministry. The information he wrote down later was from what Peter told him, from Peter's remembrances of Jesus' words.

How *should* we love God? With all our heart, soul, mind and strength.

That's really comprehensive, and that's how we should love God, with all our being. It's not really difficult to love Him when we think how grateful we are to Him for all He has done for us. However, we can know this with our intellect, but having the knowledge about something can be quite different from feeling it in our hearts. Perhaps we need to consider whether that knowledge has remained purely intellectual and only on the edge of our consciousness or whether it is something that we have allowed to sink in, to really permeate our minds and become part of our psyche, which we can express with our whole hearts, souls, minds and strengths when we talk to God, and in our praising, too.

Now here's something else that I've thought about and find absolutely fascinating. I wonder if you will see it this way, too:

---

[14] Mark 12.30 (ESV)

Have you noticed that the extra phrase in St. Mark's Gospel adds a fourth dimension to the commandment? We're familiar with the terms 2D, for two-dimensional to describe something that shows height and width, and 3D, which adds depth and makes a figure realistic and more lifelike. Now we could liken St. Mark's addition on how we can love God to what some scientists propose, such as 'time,' which is unified with the 3D concept of space. This 4D unification is said to be modern and is known as the Minkowski continuum called spacetime. Our God is eternal, His love is for all time and we read way back in Ecclesiastes,

'...there is nothing new under the sun.'[15]

In several places in the Old Testament[16] we read that we should love the Lord with all our strength, with our whole being, so it is in St. Mark's Gospel that we find God's love is all-encompassing: its width, height, depth and that it is for all time, for eternity. God had already created 4D at the beginning of time, as we know it!

When we accept that His love for us is not fickle as human love can be, we can truly come to the realization that it is absolute and forever. Then, through the power of the Holy Spirit, we can open our hearts to Him and allow it to immerse us to the very core of our being. We really feel His love for us, each of us personally, and want to express our love for Him with everything we have all of the time.

---

[15] Ecclesiastes 1.9 (ESV)

[16] For example, Deuteronomy 6.5

Now, we feel that we should be capable of loving Him like this for always, but sadly we often become involved in the things of the world and fall well short. While God continues to love us and does not change, our love for Him can fade away until we completely forget Him in the busyness of our lives. Then something gently prompts us, reminding us of our right priorities and we are led back to Him. We return, sorrowing that we have strayed, ask His forgiveness through our dear Lord Jesus and begin to experience joy again in telling God how much we love Him.

Then we need to follow that up by *showing* that we love Him.

How can I show that love?
If I love God, I can show it in the way that I live my life. In St. Mark's Gospel, the next verse continues,

> *'You shall love your neighbour as yourself.'*[17]

We can show our love for God in the way that we love other people and in the manner in which we serve and minister to them.

There are so many different approaches we can use to do this, including sharing God's love with our neighbours who are close at hand, but as the saying goes: 'All the world is a village.' As part of that global village we can show our love for God in caring for those in need all around the world.

---

[17] Mark 12.31 (ESV)

- We can pray for people, especially those whom disaster has struck, whether it is natural disaster or as a result of circumstances in the natural world, violence, terrorism, war or clumsily conceived government decisions that we see as a backward step.

- If we are in a situation where we can bring relief to people in need personally through monetary support, by going there, by bringing their plight to the attention of our government or other responsible authorities, we should do so; it is a way that we can show our love both for our neighbours and for God.

Loving yourself

Finally, we also need to remember the last word in that statement:

'...love your neighbour as ***yourself.****'*

'Yourself' implies that what God loves is worthy. Paul tells us that our bodies are the temple of God.[18] If He loves us and His Spirit dwells in us, then we should respect ourselves and care for our bodies that He has created.

f. **WHAT** is love? What words for love do we find in the Bible?

These are such hugely important questions, that we need to digress and spend some time trying to decide what love is, to see if it can be defined. We have already thought about some short descriptions of love in references in the Bible. Now we will look a little more deeply at some of the things that the Bible has to say about love. Does the Bible view love as always being the same, or does it include different kinds of love?

DISCUSSION

1. Is there a way of showing your love for God that especially stands out for you at this time?
2. When you read or recite the prayer-book liturgy, do you really think about the words that you say?
3. What is the most important way for you to show your love for God in your daily life?
4. How helpful do you find the notion of the fourth dimension in guiding you to understand the ways that we can love God?
5. In what ways can we show our love for our neighbours?

Prayer

Dear Heavenly Father, we pray that we may learn how to love You with our whole heart and our neighbours as ourselves. Thank you for the great example we have in the way Your Son showed His love for all humankind. May the Holy Spirit fill our lives so that we might follow His leading. In His Name we pray. Amen.

CHAPTER FOUR

WHAT IS LOVE?

When some people think of love, they often picture in their minds images of love-hearts or the kind of rather steamy romantic love that can be seen nightly on our televisions or that can be read about in some novels. I have heard that the popular 'love-heart' as we know it today was first designed by Michelangelo. Apparently, with his great knowledge of human physiology, which was quite astonishing for the time he lived in, this was based on his drawings of the human heart.

The word 'love' covers such a variety of feelings. We can use it loosely and even say, "I love ice-cream." This seems to show rather a paucity of descriptions in the English language.

We do have such words as 'affection,' 'fondness', 'adoration,' 'passion', 'crush,' or even a 'liking' for something, but they can seem to be poor substitutes for what we really mean. In English we often need to attach another word, or even a phrase, to describe the kind of love that we want to express.

My dictionary tells me that 'love' is 'a strong feeling of affection,' but then it goes on to describe the different facets of love in a variety of ways and it uses several different phrases to explain the meanings. In English, we do not seem to have single words that we can use that help us to explain the different kinds of love.

It would be interesting to see what happens to this word in other languages.

Love in Some Languages

Now this is where I'm going to show my ignorance. I have a smattering of some other languages, but how I wish that I knew more.

- **French**: French is often thought to be the most romantic of languages. It is allied to Italian and Spanish, and, of course, Latin. At school we were quick to learn *Je t'aime*: I love you. Later we learned other words connected with love, such as amour, tendresse, and affectionner (v).

- **Mandarin**: *Wo ai ni,* I love you. Naturally, this was one of the first terms we learned when my husband and I went to live in Taiwan, the largest of the sixty or so islands that make up the Republic of China. Of course, properly written *Wo ai ni* should be written in Chinese characters. Later we learned that this was really a phrase constructed by English speakers who were learning the language and Taiwanese people do not really say this at all, except when mimicking what foreigners say.

As in English, in Mandarin there are several phrases, or groups (usually two) of characters that express mother-love, love for God, fall in love and love of something inanimate, such as ice-cream.

- **Dobuan:** *Ya obobomeyo*, I love you. This is one of several languages spoken in the D'Entrecasteaux, a group of islands off the Eastern tip of the Papua New Guinea mainland, where we once lived many years ago.

  It is especially interesting to note that in the language of the Dobu people there are two words for a gift; one is when a gift is given and a return gift (bigger and better) is expected; the second word, *oboboma,* is also a word for a gift given in love, but the presentation of a reciprocal gift would be an insult.

- **Dutch**: When attending Melbourne High School as a lad, my husband did not learn a language apart from English. A few years later when he wanted to gain entrance to the University of Melbourne, he found he needed a language, so enrolled at Taylor's Coaching College. As I helped him learn the required vocabulary, I learned a little, too. He continued studying Dutch at university and later discovered that it was useful for translating into English some works that were found to be important in the education of the deaf.

  All that was a long time ago, and living languages change. What my husband often said to me was: *Ik heb leif von jou*, I love you. I was recently told that the way it should be said these days is *Ik hou van jou,* or *Ik heb jou life.*

- **Greek**: From my limited knowledge, Greek seems to have the most descriptive single words for love: *eros, phileo, storge,* and *agape*. Each one of these words clearly describes a different facet of love.

Love in the Bible

So what love words do we find in the Bible?

Sadly, my knowledge of Hebrew, the main language of the Old Testament Scriptures, Aramaic and the Greek of the New Testament is practically non-existent, yet these are the most important languages of the Bible, so we need to find some other sources to help us understand what is being said about love in the Bible.

The Old Testament

Most of the Old Testament was written in Hebrew, although some was in Aramaic. Theologian Professor Cranfield[19] tells us that

[19] The Reverend Professor Charles E. B. Cranfield (1915-2015) of Durham, in Alan Richardson, ed. 1957. A Theological Word Book of the Bible. London: SCM Press.

- *aheb* is a Hebrew root that occurs over 200 times in the Old Testament. It covers a wide range of meanings from love of God for people, love of people for God, passionate love, love within a family, love between friends, and love between people, when it is seen as a religious duty.

Other Hebrew words describing love in the Old Testament include

- *agab* (doting)
- *dod* ('beloved', especially found in the Song of Solomon)
- *racham*, meaning 'tender mercy'

These words are mostly connected with inward, personal feelings.

Note: The Hebrew word for beloved is written דוד. As the central letter is a sign for a vowel, it is sometimes pronounced *dud*, but this word actually means jar. I rather like that notion: that, if we allow it, God's love can fill us right up. It reminds me of the story of Elijah and the widow (1 Kings 17): the jar was filled with flour and no matter how much was taken out and shared, it never became empty. We can follow that analogy through, that no matter how much of God's love we share with others, our supply will never run out. Praise God!

The New Testament

By the way, before I begin I must tell you about this photo of a rather battered New Testament, as it's special for me. It was one of so many that were given to the lads going off overseas to fight in World War I. Dad had it with him the whole time he was away and brought it back when he came home, too.

The New Testament, as we know it, was written in classical Greek. I have read that in the New Testament there is no use of the Greek word *storge* and little of *eros*; the words mostly used by the early Christian writers are related to *phileo* and *agape*, although some other terms have also been translated into English as 'love.'

The love words in the New Testament often seem to describe feelings and attitudes that are still personal, but, as we have seen, these may go out from God to us, and from us back to Him and out to other people.

God is Love

A well-known adage tells us: 'Love is what makes the world go around,' but I guess it's really God's love for His creation and His people (even when we are not very loving of Him or of each other) that really keeps it going around. There is still so much more to learn about the different types of love and how we can use God's precious gift of love in the best way possible.

After all, we can study how human understanding has developed through the ages as God has gradually revealed the wonder of love to us, from the Old Testament Ten Commandments, in which God called His people to love Him,[20] to the New Testament where we read in the First Letter of John that *'God is love',*[21] and that perceptive passage in Mark's Gospel where the scribe replied to Jesus:

> *'You are right, Teacher. You have truly said that he is one, and there is no other beside him. And to love*

---

[20] Deuteronomy 6.5

[21] I John 4.8

> *Him with all the heart and with all the understanding and with all the strength, and to love one's neighbor as oneself, is much more than all whole burnt offerings and sacrifices.'*[22]

The New Testament includes several of Paul's Letters and his writing can be very helpful in showing us God's love and how we can love Him in return.

In Paul's letters he asks many questions and one of these is a type we haven't looked at yet. It was delivered by orators in ancient times and used in rhetoric to stress a point. With these questions, hearers in the crowd were unable to respond and orators were well aware of this and made good use of the strategy and the advantage it gave, as some of our parliamentarians and preachers continue to do today. Paul used such questions in his letters and as his readers could not respond immediately, we call them '*rhetorical questions.*' Paul was a great orator and writer, but he didn't ask questions just for the sake of asking when people did not have the opportunity to answer, it was to lead his readers to think more deeply about their faith, and these writings remains relevant for us today.

The Christian religion is not one that expects its believers to follow blindly. The faith that Paul wrote about was a believing confidence or trust in the love of God. He expected his readers to use the brains that our great Creator endowed them with, so that they could learn more about the character of God and His love.

In his Letters, Paul expects his readers, and that includes us today, to follow Jesus' example and live a Christian life, having fellowship with God, and by making decisions

[22] Mark 12.32 – 33 (ESV)

wisely throughout our lives, in the strength of the Holy Spirit.

Another way

Perhaps if we examine the question another way, it would help to throw more light on what seemed, at first, to be a simple query that required a simple answer. This alternate way would be to unpack the question and look at each of its components to try and understand its essential nature.

DISCUSSION

1. In what other languages can you say, 'I love you'? When you translate these words in the other language back into English, do they tell us the same thing?
2. If the Old Testament word for God, YHWH, is actually made up of all vowels in Hebrew, and there is only one marker to signify a vowel, how should this word be pronounced?[23]
3. What do we mean when we say that God's love is a gift to us?
4. In what ways can we have fellowship with God?
5. What does the wording on the red banner above mean for you? Do you think that it has any special meaning for us as Christians?

[23] It cannot be pronounced as no one now knows how the vowels were to be said

Prayer

Dear Father God, we praise you for your great love for us. May our love for you rise like incense and the perfume spread to those around us, so that others may catch this love, not by our words only, but also by our example in the way we live our lives, modeling them on the life of love and caring shown to us in your Son, Jesus Christ. In His name we pray. Amen.

NOTES

CHAPTER FIVE

UNPACKING THE QUESTION

1. GOD

Do you love God?

There are so many questions we can ask when we want to find out more about loving God. The question appears simple, but there are so many ramifications that it's not so simple to answer. 'Yes' is not nearly enough. Such a question definitely requires a more comprehensive reply.

To help us unpack our question and look at what is implied here, we can examine more carefully those few brief words by looking at the question backwards:

GOD LOVE YOU DO

Beginning with God

Now we are getting onto the right track as we are putting God first instead of ourselves or anything or anyone else. The first Book of the Bible, *Genesis*, puts God first; it commences the whole of the Bible Scriptures with the words:

> *'In the beginning God...'*[24]

For Christians, and for those who love Him, God comes first, so we must ask the question:

[24] Genesis 1.1 (KJV)

Who is God?

When we ask this question and search the Scriptures to find an answer, we find that over the long ages covered in the Old Testament God was slowly revealing Himself to His people through the prophets and through their experiences in life. Until the advent of Jesus, when He came to live on earth as a human being, God's people did not fully understand what the prophets had been telling them; that from before the creation of the world God was and is. It's not always an easy concept for our human minds to comprehend that He is everlasting, unchanging and eternal, but in this world of constant change, turmoil, disasters, wars and rumours of wars, it's a very comforting thing to know that our great Creator has always been and always will be.

It can help our understanding of God and our relationship with Him to know that He has always been and will always be a threefold God.

THE TRINITY

As Christians, we worship what we call the Trinity, our Triune[25] God: God the Father, God the Son (Jesus Christ) and God the Holy Spirit.

To digress for a moment, if we are to know and love the God we worship, then we need to understand about the Trinity. The word is not mentioned in the Bible, but it is there in essence. God is One, but He is also three distinct Persons at

[25] This means 'three in one'

the same time. He speaks of Himself as *'I AM'*, but as early as the first chapter of Genesis, He says,

> *'Let US make man in OUR image'* (Genesis 1. 26, ESV).

That revelation introduces us to the concept that God is made up of more than one. As He reveals Himself more and more as we progress through the Scriptures we find there are many examples of God as Three Persons, for example:

FATHER: In the Book of Isaiah in the Old Testament we find that God is called 'Father' several times, as in Isaiah 63.16 (KJV):

> *'Thou, O Lord, art our Father,'*

and in Matthew 5.44 - 45 (ESV) in the New Testament:

> *'Love your enemies and pray for those who persecute you, so that you may be children of your **Father in heaven**.'*

SON: In Isaiah 9.6 (KJV) in the Old Testament we read the prophesy of His coming:

> *'For unto us a child is born, unto us a **son** is given ... and his name shall be called ... **The mighty God**.'*

While in the New Testament in Mark 1.11 (ESV) at the baptism of Jesus:

> *'A voice came from heaven, "You are my beloved **Son**,"'*

and in John 10.30 (ESV) Jesus said:

> *'**I** and the **Father** are **one**.'*

HOLY SPIRIT: In the Old Testament in Genesis 1.2 (KJV) we read,

> *'And the **Spirit of God** moved upon the face of the waters,'*

and in Psalm 139. 7 – 10 (KJV):

> *'Whither shall I go from **your Spirit**? Or whither shall I flee from your presence? If I ascend up into heaven, thou art there! ... thy hand shall lead me, and thy right hand shall hold me.'*

In the New Testament, Luke 4.18 (ESV) describes a time when Jesus read from Isaiah 61, but was actually referring to himself:

> *'The **Spirit of the Lord** is upon me, because he has anointed me to proclaim good news.'*

It may help our understanding of the Trinity if we hear an interesting story from another time in history when St. Patrick and his friends took Christianity to Ireland. St. Patrick wanted to explain to the people about the Trinity, and searched around to see how he could do it. God showed him the shamrock. He plucked a leaf and held it for the people to see that it was one leaf, but that it had three separate parts. That is the same with the God we worship.

To help us understand more about the Trinity, let us examine the concept in more detail in the next three chapters.

DISCUSSION

1. Do we always remember to put God first in our lives? Why should we? What happens when we don't?
2. How do we know that God is eternal?
3. 'I AM' is in the present tense. Why do you think this is so?
4. Do you think that any one Person of the Trinity is more important than the other two? Is it important for us to understand about the Trinity?
5. If you were asked to explain the Trinity, what analogy could you use?

Prayer*

May none of God's wonderful works keep silence, night or morning.

Bright stars, high mountains, the depths of the seas, sources of rushing rivers: may all these break into song as we sing to Father, Son and Holy Spirit.

May all the angels in the heavens reply: Amen! Amen! Amen!

Power, praise, honour and eternal glory to God,
the only giver of grace.

Amen! Amen! Amen!

*An Egyptian Doxology from the Third Century

NOTES

CHAPTER SIX

THE TRINITY: GOD THE FATHER

In the last chapter we found that the Old Testament of the Bible opens with the words: '*In the beginning God.*' God is eternal; He *is* and was and ever will be - yesterday, today and forever.

Isn't that wonderful! So much in this world changes, but our Father God is forever! He is constant and His love for His people is constant, too. He does not change and His love for His people does not change, either.

If we are going to put God first in our lives and trust and worship Him as our Father, we need to learn as much as we can about Him. Psalms is a good place to begin as David and the others who wrote the Psalms really knew how to love God as their Father and to trust in Him through all the vicissitudes of life. Right in Psalm 1, we meditate on the importance of learning to know the difference between good and evil. We are reminded of how blessed we can be if we delight in God's law, obey it, and continually keep it in our hearts. By so doing we will be like a tree that is planted beside an irrigation channel; even when the surrounding land is like a desert, our roots will reach deep so that we can be sustained by the waters of life that God provides. Sometimes we may have to wait until that water reaches us, but if we wait, as we read in Psalm 130.5 (KJV),

> *'I wait for the Lord, my soul doth wait, and in his word do I hope.'*

Our Father knows our need and we will receive. It may not be when we expect it, but He loves and cares for us and we can be sure that it will be the right time in His plan for our lives. God's timing is always perfect.

There are many other places in the Scriptures where we can learn about God the Father. The Scriptures are His word to us, His people. In Proverbs 30.5 (ESV) we read that '*Every word of God proves true,*' we can trust His word. Again, in Luke 8.11-15 (KJV), where Jesus explains to His disciples the parable of the seeds, He tells them that

> '*The seed is the word of God.*'

The parable continues with the dispersal of the seeds by the sower: some fall on rocks and are received with joy, but they cannot grow roots and in difficult times they fall away; seeds that fall among the thorns are choked, as people can be by the cares and riches of the world and so they do not mature, but the seeds that fall on good soil:

'*As for that in the good soil, they are those who, hearing the word, hold it fast in an honest and good heart, and bear fruit*[26] *with patience*' (Luke 8.15).

Illustration by Annie Vallotton

May it be that we are good soil, so that God's word will grow in our hearts, and when we are patient may it bear much good fruit.

---

[26] Annie Vallotton was the illustrator for the Good News Bible. Illustration used with permission from its owner, Genevieve Cutler

In the previous chapter some examples of *'God the Father'* were provided in the discussion of the Trinity. Many others can be found in both the Old Testament, as in Psalm 89.26 (ESV): *'You are my Father, my God,'* and in Isaiah 9.6 (KJV): *'The everlasting Father.'* In the New Testament, in Matthew 5.16 (ESV), we find that Jesus told His hearers,

> *'Let your light shine before others, so that they may see your good works and give glory to your Father who is in heaven.'*

In St. Mark's gospel, 11.25 (ESV) we read:

> *'Whenever you stand praying, forgive. If you have anything against anyone; so that your Father who is in heaven may forgive you your trespasses.'*

'God the Father' is mentioned in many more references throughout the Bible, but as we read and search we find that there are other names for God that tell us more, and these help us to understand more about the character of our Father God. Some of these other names are given here.

God the Father in the Old Testament

As we progress through the Books of the Old Testament we read the history (His Story) of God's relationship with His chosen people. Father God gradually reveals Himself through His names and these help to teach us more about Him:

> **Holy God** (Leviticus 19.2, KJV): *'Ye shall be holy, for I the Lord your God am holy.'*
>
> **God of gods** (Deuteronomy, 10.17, KJV): *'The Lord your God is God of gods.'*

God of Forgiveness (Nehemiah 9.17, KJV): *'But you are a God ready to pardon, gracious and merciful, slow to anger and of great kindness.'*

God of my Praise (Psalm 109.1, ESV)): *'Do not be silent, O God of my praise.'*

God of Justice (Isaiah 30.18, ESV): *'For the Lord is a God of justice; blessed are all those who wait for him.'*

Living God (Jeremiah 10.10, ESV): 'The Lord is the true God; he is the living God.'

There are many more, and these include: el Shaddai,[27] I AM,[28] The Lord God, the God of your fathers,[29] 'the Lord of hosts.'[30] YHWH,[31] and Creator.[32]

God the Father in the New Testament

Jesus referred to God as Father, and one of these stands out. It occurred when the Disciples asked Jesus to teach them how to pray and He taught them what we call *The Lord's Prayer*. It begins with *'Our Father.'* This stresses the fact that, as Christians, we are God's children. We love God as a child loves his father, but this Father is so much

---

[27] This means God Almighty; it is found 7 times in the Old Testament, the first time is in Genesis 17.1

[28] When Moses asked God His name, He replied, 'I AM.' This was in Exodus 3.14

[29] That is, Abraham, Isaac and Jacob. This is found in Exodus 3. 15

[30] Isaiah 6.3 (KJV)

[31] We usually write this as Yahweh. The name is first mentioned in Genesis 2. 4. I believe it is found 6,519 times in the Old Testament, but it is frequently translated in English as Lord God

[32] Although there is much about Creation and God creating the world, the first time the word Creator is mentioned is in Ecclesiastes 12.1 (KJV)

mightier than an earthly father. How special is that! This thought was explained further by St. Paul in his *Letter to the Ephesians* 4.6 (KJV):

> *'One God and Father of all, who is above all, and through all, and in you all.'*

I love to tell the story of when I was teaching Scripture to my class in an independent school in Melbourne: I found that the Jewish girls left out the vowels when writing YHWH, as they had been taught that God's name was too holy to write fully. Yet how often we hear people, even some of those who call themselves Christian, take the name of the Lord in vain by using the names of God, of Jesus and Christ. *'Oh My God'* has become so commonplace as OMG on mobile phones and the Internet. This is breaking the first of the important Ten Commandments[33] that God gave His people as rules to live by.

More about God the Father

He loves us

As we have seen, St. John wrote that *'God is love.'*[34]

Although many people may think that the God who is worshipped by a number of different religions is the same god, that is not so. This is one of the points where Christianity stands apart. It is reinforced by Jesus' interpretation of the Ten Commandments that we have seen in Mark 12.31. Our God is a God of love and in some other religions that claim to worship God that love is missing.

---

[33] Exodus 20.7

[34] I John 4.16 (KJV)

He is our Father in Heaven

In the Holy Bible, God's Guidebook that was written especially for us, we learn that God is our Heavenly Father, although God the Trinity is not only Father, but also Son and Holy Spirit. Jesus taught His disciples to pray to 'our Father in Heaven,' but the phrase 'Heavenly Father' is not found in the Scriptures.

We are His Children

If we claim, through Jesus, that God is our Father in Heaven, then we become His children, and what an honour and joy that is! There are several references to this in the New Testament, including

> *'For ye are all the children of God by faith in Christ Jesus.'*[35]

> *'It is evident who are the children of God, and who are the children of the devil: whoever does not practise righteousness is not of God...'*[36]

That's saying it straight, isn't it? It is only through putting our faith and trust in Jesus that we can become children of God.

Love in our Family

That last verse from I John 3.10 concludes:

> *'...nor are those who do not love their brothers and sister.'*[37]

---

[35] Galatians 3.26 (KJV)
[36] I John 3.10 (ESV)
[37] 1 John 3.10 (NRSV)

If we are 'of God', if we are His children, then others who put their faith in Jesus and become children of God are our brothers and sisters, and we should love them. Together we are part of God's family.

God Cares for Us

Our Father in Heaven loves and cares for us. He knows our needs. We can read about this in many of the Books of the Bible; in the Old Testament we find this loving care in many places, but especially in the Psalms. That familiar and much loved Psalm 23 (KJV) begins with the words:

> *'The Lord is my shepherd; I shall not want.'*

Almost the whole of Psalm 139 is a prayer of praise for God's care, and further:

'No good thing will he withhold from them that walk uprightly.'[38]

A gift from the ladies in the office, Good Shepherd Church, Taiwan

In the New Testament, there is a passage of Jesus' words to His disciples that is so special to me, Matthew 10.28 – 32. One day when I was on my way to school when I was ten

[38] Psalm 84.11b (KJV)

years old I had such a frightening experience. I was running late and took a forbidden short cut up a laneway. There I saw a woman lying dead with blood and a knife sticking in her chest. I was terrified. I arrived late and the Christian Religious Instruction teacher, Miss Stephenson, was just speaking about this passage. 'Fear not them which kill the body' (Matthew 10.28, KJV). She told us that God truly cares for each person, big or small, rich or poor. He knows when the tiniest sparrow dies, and we're worth much more to Him than many small birds. He cares for us so much that He knows everything about us, even the number of hairs on our heads. If we give our lives to Jesus and tell other people about how He died to save us from our sins, then He will remind our Father in heaven that we love Him and when we die we will go to live with Him forever.

That was the catalyst for my 'born again' experience. I couldn't wait until school finished. I tore home as fast as I could, knelt down in my Mother's fernery under the tree-fern and gave my life to Jesus.

There are many other verses which tell us of God's care for us, such as Luke 12.20 – 31, and that lovely verse in 1 Peter 5.7 (KJV), which tells us what to do when we feel loaded with problems:

> *'Casting all your care upon him; for he careth for you.'*

DISCUSSION

1. Have you ever experienced the surety that God's timing is perfect? How did that affect your relationship with Him as Father in heaven?
2. What can we do to spread the good seed of God's word?
3. Why do we refer to the Bible as God's Guidebook?
4. How can it be evident that we are children of God?
5. In what ways can we practise the righteousness of God?

Prayer

Dear Father in Heaven thank you that you really care for us. Thank you for the great privilege of being called your children. Help us to live holy, righteous lives, so that we may be worthy of that name. Bless us with the light of your countenance and grace us with a childlike trust, so that we know your love and peace in our lives. We pray in Jesus' wonderful Name. Amen.

NOTES

CHAPTER SEVEN

THE TRINITY: GOD THE SON

When God's Son was born, His earthly parents chose the name they had been told to give their baby, in accordance with the instructions of an angel. In Luke 1.26, we read that the name of this angel was Gabriel. Angels are God's messengers. In the *'Book of Daniel'* (which was written long ago in the sixth century B.C.), we read that Gabriel is the angel whose work it is to reveal. That is just what he did before their baby was born. We can read about it in St. Luke's Gospel, where we are told that Gabriel revealed to Mary, saying:

> *'...you shall call his name Jesus.'*[39]

Later an angel came to Joseph in a dream and told him the same thing, but he also defined the meaning of the name and the purpose of His coming:

> *'Thou shalt call his name Jesus; for he shall save his people from their sins.'*[40]

In the Old Testament

In fact, if we read on further in St. Matthew's gospel we find that this had been foretold hundreds of years before in Isaiah 7.14 (KJV). He quotes:

> *'Behold a virgin shall conceive and bear a son, and shall call his name Immanuel.'*

Matthew then explained,

---

[39] Luke 1.31 (ESV)
[40] Matthew 1.21 (KJV)

'...which being interpreted is, God with us.'[41]

It was part of God's plan for the redemption of our sinful world. Centuries before Jesus was born on earth, God made a covenant with His people through the prophets of old that a Saviour would come to save His chosen people. As well as that promise we have looked at in Isaiah, we find many references to the prediction of His coming in the Old Testament. It's said that there are over three hundred references. In John 5.46 (ESV), Jesus Himself referred to these prophecies when speaking to Jewish people:

'For if you believed Moses, you would believe me; for he wrote of me.'

Among several other names given to describe Jesus in Old Testament prophecies, He was also named as

'Wonderful, Counsellor...The Prince of Peace'.[42]

Although the prophets spoke and wrote about the promised Messiah as *Prince of Peace*, the people of God, who were often at war with neighbouring countries, expected Him to be a war-like leader who would save them from their current enemies round about, rather than from their sins that were within.

---

41 Matthew 1.23b (KJV)
42 Isaiah 9.6 (KJV)

Sometimes when we read about the many battles that are described in the Old Testament, we wonder why God allowed His chosen people to be involved in so many dreadful disasters. It was precisely because they kept forgetting about God, or intentionally turned their backs on Him, as they changed to loving, worshipping and sacrificing to lifeless man-made idols instead of seeking God to ask for forgiveness of their sins. God allowed these calamities to occur, to remind His people to turn back to Him; that He alone was the one to be loved and worshipped. So often they would turn back for a while, but then forget again.

There are many references to the days leading up to the Crucifixion of Jesus in the Old Testament, such as the foretelling of the tragedy of Judas' betrayal in Zechariah 11.13, and of the Crucifixion itself, as in Zechariah 12.10 and especially the foreshadowing of Christ's death in Psalm 22. Other prophecies concerning Jesus include His resurrection in Psalm 16.10 and the Ascension in Psalm 68.18.

In the New Testament

As God revealed Himself gradually to His people through His actions and the names He gave Himself in the Old Testament, so in the New Testament we can read Jesus' statements about Himself and these include names that help us to understand His mission during His ministry on earth, and this is still relevant for us today.

In St. Matthew's Gospel, we find that Jesus Himself affirmed to His disciples that He was *'the Messiah, the Son of the living God.'*[43]

The word, *Messiah*, is a Hebrew word and means 'Anointed One.' In Greek it is *Christ*.

All four Gospels mention times when Jesus referred to prophecies concerning Himself in the Old Testament, for example, when He explained the Scriptures to the sad Christians who were walking together on their way to Emmaus after the Crucifixion:

> *'And beginning at Moses and all the prophets, he expounded unto them in all the scriptures the things concerning himself.'*[44]

We may remember that the Old Testament Scriptures describe how Moses led the Children of Israel during their exodus from Egypt. For forty years they travelled in the wilderness on their way to a permanent home in the Promised Land. During this long time, God's wayward children learned more about their Father, God. When Moses asked God His name at this time, He replied,

> ***"I AM."***[45]

Interestingly, the names Jesus gave Himself link Him with God, pointing to His divinity, as each of the seven statements about Jesus that are recorded in John's gospel begin with "I AM:"

> *'I am the bread of life'* [46]

> *'I am the light of the world'* [47]

---

[43] Matthew 16.16 (NRSV)
[44] Luke 24. 27 (KJV)
[45] Exodus 3.14 (KJV)
[46] John 6. 35 (KJV)

'I am the door of the sheep'[48]

'I am the good shepherd'[49]

'I am the resurrection and the life' [50]

'I am the way, the truth and the life' [51]

'I am the true vine' [52]

Jesus was pointing out that He is the Son of God, Messiah of the world and our everlasting Saviour.

The name 'Jesus' is the Greek form of the Hebrew name 'Joshua.' Some of the early church leaders saw in His name a parallel between Joshua who, in the Old Testament led God's people into the Promised Land after Moses died, and Jesus who, in the New Testament leads God's people to the everlasting Kingdom.

These "I AM" names that Jesus gave Himself can be very helpful in aiding our understanding of His various functions as part of the Trinity, but the most important for us today is when we see Him as our Saviour and Messiah.

Just as the people of the Old Testament turned their backs on God, so His people of the New Covenant did not understand that Jesus had not come as an earthly king to save them from their enemies. By this time, the traditional sacrifices that were required for the forgiveness of their sins were often carried out in a way that had become meaningless. Jesus, the One without sin, willingly gave

---

[47] John 8. 12 (KJV)
[48] John 10. 7 (KJV)
[49] John 10. 11 (KJV)
[50] John 11. 25 (KJV)
[51] John 14. 6 (KJV)
[52] John 15. 1 (KJV)

Himself in the place of the sacrificial 'Lamb without blemish' and became the once-for-all sacrifice for the forgiveness of our sins. He loved God's people so much, and that includes us, that He was willing to undergo that pain and anguish. When we accept that sacrifice and put our trust and faith in Jesus, God forgives our sins. Then we are purified, made holy and righteous, and this enables us to come close to the Great "I AM" who is so pure and holy, and have the wonderful privilege of fellowship with Him and the promise of life with Him forever, eternally!

Through our acceptance of God's great gift of love and our confirmation of Jesus as our personal Saviour, we find our way to true and eternal life. How could we not love Him?

DISCUSSION

1. We have Christmas when we celebrate the birth of Jesus and Easter when we remember His death and resurrection. Are there any other special days in our Christian calendar when we celebrate events concerned with Jesus?
2. Do you believe that the writings in the Old Testament that we say are about Jesus were really prophecies, or do we read too much into these Scriptures? Why?
3. What do the words 'New Testament' mean?
4. Can you think of any other 'I AM' phrases that help us to understand the character of Jesus?
5. How can we show our thanks to Jesus for His great love and all He has done for us?

Prayer

Thank you dear Jesus for the joy of being truly alive in your love. Unite us in fellowship with you and with each other as we journey in hope towards everlasting life through your great sacrifice for the forgiveness of our sins. Amen.

NOTES

CHAPTER EIGHT

THE TRINITY: GOD THE HOLY SPIRIT

The Work of the Holy Spirit in the Old Testament

God first mentions His Spirit in Genesis 1. 2. That's right at the beginning of the Bible and the beginning of the description of the creation of the world. Not much further on, in 6. 3 we are told that the Spirit will dwell in human beings until they die, when the Spirit will leave them.

As one of the Persons of the Trinity, the Holy Spirit is also fully God. He convicts people of their sin and when they give their lives to God He comes and lives in them, giving them power to live holy and faithful lives; He supports in time of trouble and aids us in understanding the Scriptures. The Holy Spirit is known as Comforter and Guide, including the guiding of the writers of the Bible as they recorded the words of God. He took the form of a dove at Jesus' baptism.

Among other things that tell us in the Bible about the Holy Spirit, we find that He is described as both breath and power.

Breath

In the early Scriptures the Spirit was often thought of as 'breath.' In Genesis 2.7 we read that man only became a living being after *God* breathed into his nostrils the breath of life. This also tells us that the Holy Spirit is one of the Persons of the Trinity. We're also told that Job claimed that the breath of the Spirit would maintain his integrity despite all his problems:

> *'As long as my breath is in me, and the spirit of God is in my nostrils.'*[53]

We find further on in The Book of Job more about the Holy Spirit as breath:

> *'It is the spirit in man, the breath of the Almighty that makes him understand.'*[54]

It is in breathing in and being filled with the Holy Spirit that we find our inspiration in the life He has given us. Praise Him for this great gift.

In the Nicene Creed[55] that we traditionally recite each Sunday, we state that we believe in the Holy Spirit as Lord and giver of life. This notion is sometimes carried further. It suggests that, if only we will do so, inviting the Holy Spirit to dwell in us is as easy as inhaling, and in doing so we also inhale God's love. Then we find that when we exhale we share God's love; through inspiration and expiration we can inspire others with His Spirit of love, too.

---

[53] Job 27.3 (ESV)

[54] Job 32.8 (ESV); also *see* Job 33.4

[55] This creed was adopted by the First Council of bishops in Nicaea, which met in 325 in the city of Nicaea (in Turkey today).

Power

The Hebrews saw the Holy Spirit as being very important as the *power* of God and that it was through this power that God revealed Himself to them. It can be the same for us. The message that the life of humankind is due to the power of the Spirit can be found in several Books of the Old Testament, but it is especially clear in Ezekiel's description of his revelation from God.[56] It is good to read the whole passage. It ends with verse 14:

> *'And [I] shall put my spirit in you, and ye shall live.'*

With the infilling of the Holy Spirit in our lives we really live!

Other Old Testament references to the power of the Holy Spirit include Jeremiah 6.11, Isaiah 58.1, Ezekiel 23.36, Micah 1.5, and in 3.8 Micah wrote:

> *'I am full of power by the Spirit of the Lord.'*

May we all be filled with that power of the Holy Spirit so that we can join the prophets and have the strength to speak out about the injustices that we see being committed around us in the world today.

The Holy Spirit and Prophecy in the Old Testament

The Holy Spirit Warns Against Danger

The work of the Holy Spirit can be seen in the Old Testament in the books of the Spirit when they warned the people of coming disasters if they did not mend their

[56] Ezekiel 37. 3 – 14 (KJV)

ways.[57] How often His people wandered away and forgot about God!

Sadly, even today after all we have learned, we often continue along that path, trying to 'go it alone' and end up with our lives in disaster mode.

The Holy Spirit Gives Revelation

Again, we state in the Nicene Creed[58] which many of us recite each Sunday, that

> *'We believe in the Holy Spirit, the Lord, the giver of life, who proceeds from the Father and the Son, who with the Father and the Son is worshipped and glorified, who has spoken through the prophets.'*

He has spoken down the centuries through the prophets. The Holy Spirit guided and inspired the prophets and writers of old to gradually reveal the coming of the Messiah in the Old Testament. This is especially evident in Isaiah[59] where God promises to pour His Spirit on His children and their descendants.

When we come to the *Book of the Prophet Ezekiel* we find that God is moving from caring for the external needs of His people. Instead, He promises to cleanse them internally, giving them a new heart and a new spirit.[60] But they needed to wait until the advent of the Messiah, for that to happen.

---

[57] For example, Nehemiah 9.30
[58] See, for example, in 'A Prayer Book for Australia,' p. 123
[59] 44.3
[60] Ezekiel 36.25 - 27

The Work of the Holy Spirit in the New Testament

Power and Breath

In the New Testament we find that the Holy Spirit remains involved with God's power. Jesus promised that if we love Him, the Holy Spirit would live in us forever:

> *'And I will pray the Father, and he shall give you another Comforter, that he may abide with you for ever.'*[61]

This fits with the first mention of the Holy Spirit in Genesis. God has given us the power of choice and if we choose to accept, through Jesus, God's gift of eternal life, we are filled with the 'breath of God,' then when our mortal bodies expire we will live in the Spirit eternally. But remember, it is our choice and our whole future depends on it.

Baptism of the Holy Spirit

The experience of the Holy Spirit in the Old Testament is revealed to a much greater extent in the New Testament. We see this especially in *The Acts of the Apostles.*[62] Jesus had instructed the Apostles to wait for this experience to occur. They were gathered together in Jerusalem for the festival of Pentecost, which was harvest festival time, fifty days after Passover, and came together for prayer and fellowship as they waited. This time the Holy Spirit

---

[61] John 14.16 (KJV)

[62] Acts 2.2 - 4

descended on them in fulfillment of Jesus' promise, firstly as the sound of a rushing wind and then as tongues of fire and it was poured out on all the Apostles:

> *'And they were all filled with the Holy Ghost, and began to speak with other tongues, as the Spirit gave them utterance.'*[63]

The filling with the Holy Spirit at Pentecost was an amazing occurrence that was the catalyst for the inception of the Church. It was from shortly after this time that the followers of Jesus became known as Christians.[64]

The Holy Spirit Living in Us

Let us think about the *First Epistle of Paul the Apostle to the Thessalonians* as he discussed the ideal way to live the Christian life. Near the end of his letter Paul wrote:

> *'...give thanks in all circumstances; for this is the will of God in Christ Jesus for you. Do not quench the Spirit. Do not despise prophecies but test everything; hold fast to what is good.'*[65]

When we become Christians and invite the Holy Spirit to live in us, we have so much for which we can thank and praise God. That is important all life long, but it is only part of the true Spirit-filled life. We need to be careful. Paul warns that we do not receive the Spirit so we can live for that alone, we are to be active and responsible, accountable to God Himself, in discriminating between what is good and what is bad. All through our lives we must cling to what is good and then make it known. When

---

[63] Acts 2.4 (KJV)
[64] Acts 11.26
[65] 1 Thessalonians 5.18 – 21 (ESV)

the Spirit reveals these things to our hearts, just as He revealed them to the prophets of old, we have a responsibility to share this knowledge with others.

Let us not forget the importance of the Holy Spirit. He is, among other things:

- Our Guide through life
- Our Helper[66]
- Our Advocate[67]
- Our Counsellor[68]
- Our Comforter[69] (the word 'Comforter' is often translated as 'Helper')
- Our Teacher[70]
- Our Spirit of Truth,[71] helping us to discern what is good, and what is evil.

---

66 John 14.16 (ESV)
67 I John 2.1(KJV)
68 Isaiah 9.6 (KJV)
69 John 14.16 (KJV)
70 John 14.26 (KJV)
71 John 16.13 (KJV)

DISCUSSION

1. How can we balance our inspiration and expiration of God's love through the Holy Spirit?
2. Are there things in our lives that might grieve the Holy Spirit?
3. How can we understand the Person of the Holy Spirit through His presence in believers?
4. Why do we call God's Spirit Holy?
5. How are the ascension of Jesus and the Holy Spirit related?

Prayer

Dear Lord, may we accept and use the gift of the Holy Spirit wisely in every area of our lives. May He be active as our Guide to make all things new all the way on our journey here on Earth as we strive to attain eternal life with You. Praise you, Father for this great gift. We pray through Jesus Christ.
Amen.

CHAPTER NINE

LOVING AND WORSHIPPING GOD

When we give thanks to God and worship Him we show how we honour and celebrate our love for Him in the way that we praise Him. Our worship expresses our great respect, gratitude and joy for all He has done for us and for all that He *is* for us; we know He is the Great I AM.

It is true that we can worship and praise God at home in our private prayer and praise and in our daily Quiet Time, and some people will try to tell us that that is sufficient, there is no need to go to church services. However, we must not forget that corporate worship is important. 'Corporate' means 'Body', and as a member of the Body of Christ, we need to worship Him together.

Worship is a time of unity with other Christians. In our Eucharist the priest says:

> '*We who are many are one body.*' [72]

Then we say together with the other people in church,

> '*For we all share in the one Bread.*' [73]

This is taken from the '*Letter of Paul to the Romans.*'

---

[72] Romans 12.5 (NRSV)

[73] See p. 37; Jesus is the Bread of life

The Church building where we worship may be very beautiful and may have been a house of prayer for many years, or it might be quite a humble building, but it is not the building that is important; the true church is God's people wherever we meet, when as a body we worship and praise Him together.

The Chapel at St. John's University, Taiwan

We are members of Christ's body, but we are all different. Did you know that although the population of the earth is so vast, every person on it is unique, just as the respective members of our bodies are different and were created for specific purposes? It's the fact that we, as Christians, are together in the one body. That is what is important - and how, wherever we are, we use the talents that God has given us, to be the best member that we can be of that body.

That reminds me of a story about a little boy who was taken to his aunt's funeral. Looking at the flower bedecked coffin, he whispered rather loudly to his mother,

"What's in the box, Mum?"

"That's Auntie Irene's body."

There was a pause for thought; then the loud whisper came again,

"Well, where's her head?"

Funny, but what a wonderful reminder! We may be members of the body of Christ, the Church, but we must never forget that He is the Head. We are not perfect and so no church is perfect; we cannot work together unless we keep in constant contact with the Head, allowing Him to direct our ways.

That is why it is so good to develop the habit of regular corporate worship with other Christians, to share our love for God – Father, Son and Holy Spirit.

Habits – Good and Bad

A habit, as we all know, is a tendency we find in ourselves to act in a certain way, and we keep repeating that act, whether it is good or bad.

Bad Habits

We often think of a habit as being something we do in our lives that's not so good, even downright sinful and we come to the realization that we should concentrate in prayer to work on it with vigour to eradicate it. For most people, and especially for those who love God, we may be aware of the fact that, whether we like it or not, we have developed some habits that are not good, not for us and not for those around us. We have fallen into a rut and, much to our chagrin, we find ourselves repeating this bad habit over and over again.

We know that we need to strive to overcome this habit, even when that is difficult or seems absolutely impossible.

Perhaps we cannot overcome this annoying habit as much as we try to in our own strength, but if we turn to our Lord God for help we can be assured that we can be forgiven through God the Son and achieve our goal with the strength and power of His Holy Spirit.

Good Habits

Conversely, we may really desire to develop good habits. This may not be easy either, but it's a worthwhile, positive thing to attempt, and what a joy it is when we succeed! Again we need to be in fellowship with our Lord God if we are to succeed in this endeavour.

Like many other Christians, for some years in my spiritual life I have striven to develop a good habit, in the hope that it may help to eradicate a bad one – and there are plenty of those! This particular good habit is one that I concentrate on in order to help me grow in my inner, spiritual life. Then I can hope to accomplish my aim and share the fruit of this good habit with others.

This method of mine may not work for you because, as we have seen, each person is different and unique, and we all have different ways of learning as we strive to become more Christ-like in the way we live our lives.

What I believe that God has asked me to do at these times is to decide to choose one of St. Paul's Fruit of the Spirit[74] that he wrote about to that wayward community of ancient Celts, called Galatians.[75]

---

[74] Galatians 5: 22-23 (ESV)

[75] *See* pp. 185 – 198 in Bronwen Scott-Branagan, 2014, St. Paul's Letter to the Celts.

I choose a fruit that God has shown me is very needful of improvement in my life at that particular time, and together with my Father God and in the strength of the Holy Spirit I work on it in prayer and meditation to cultivate this good habit. This method of developing a good habit may work for you, too. It's certainly worth a try!

There are nine of Paul's fruit altogether:

Love,

joy,

peace,

patience,

kindness,

goodness,

faithfulness,

gentleness,

self-control

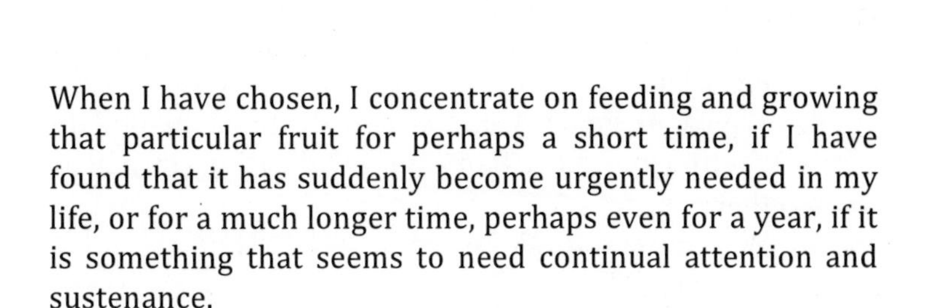

When I have chosen, I concentrate on feeding and growing that particular fruit for perhaps a short time, if I have found that it has suddenly become urgently needed in my life, or for a much longer time, perhaps even for a year, if it is something that seems to need continual attention and sustenance.

Try it! It really helps to focus on areas that need that cultivation. It's a positive action to take and our Christian lives can be so much better for the thought and prayer that we have bestowed on it.

Notice how St. Paul puts *love* as the first of these fruits.

DISCUSSION

1. What makes it important that we should go to church to worship God? The people we see at church aren't perfect.
2. What is the meaning of 'corporate' worship?
3. Which bad habit in your life would it be good to eradicate?
4. Which of Paul's fruits would be most helpful in sharing our Christian story with others? Why is that?
5. Why do you think Paul put love as the first in his list of fruit?

Prayer

Holy Spirit, it is only with your love, guidance and power that we can cleanse our lives of bad habits. Breathe on us now and give us the strength that we need to put these things away from us and to replace them with good habits so that we may bring forth good fruit in our lives. Praise you Lord, that what may have seemed impossible in our own strength can be made possible in you. We pray in the name of Jesus. Amen.

NOTES

CHAPTER TEN

UNPACKING THE QUESTION

2. LOVE

Firstly, we shall again ask questions: Does our love and awareness of God grow slowly, or does it occur suddenly? What is love? What are the different types of love?

Do you love God?

In our original question the word 'love' is used as a verb. When we were at school we probably learned that a verb is a 'doing word.' Loving is something that we *do*, and it's defined as having a strong liking or affection for someone or something. We know from experience that this particular verb is connected with our feelings, our emotions.

It is very difficult for us to stand back from our love and look at it objectively, whether it is for God or for something or someone else. That is because our love is an emotion or rather a whole complex of emotions, and this causes us to be actively involved. We love, even when we do not know or understand how it came about. Can we say that of the way in which we love God? Did it just happen as we grew to know Him more? How involved are we in our love for Him?

Growth or Revelation

Did our love for God grow slowly or was it a sudden revelation of just how much God loves us, and what it means in the whole of our lives?

Growth

Perhaps our love for God grew imperceptibly from our earliest childhood memories of learning about Him from our parents and in our church community. Then it may have continued to grow until it blossomed when we reached sufficient maturity to be able to confirm that love in a special way, possibly in a service at church. That growth may have been developing slowly over a number of years as we learned more about Him.

It is not always that way.

Revelation

Perhaps our experience of God's love stems from a time when we suddenly realized just what His love means in our life and we had a special 'born again' experience, a revelation. That was the time when we gave that life back to our Creator with the decision to live within His will as much as ever we could. Jesus said, '*Unless one is born again he cannot see the kingdom of God*,'[76] and later in this discourse:

> '*That which is born of the flesh is flesh, and that which is born of the Spirit is spirit.*'[77]

---

[76] John 3.3 (ESV)
[77] John 3.6 (KJV)

Growth and Revelation

For me, a combination of both is needed: *growth* as we learn, until we receive a *revelation,* a special time when we feel the urgency or deep desire to give our lives to God through Jesus, who gave His life on the cross for us. For me, to be a true Christian means that a 'born again' experience is essential; it is the only way.

Do you remember reading about Nicodemus who was a Pharisee, a member of the Sanhedrin and an important teacher of Israel? He secretly visited Jesus in the middle of the night. We can read about this in John 3. 1-21. This passage includes that much loved and quoted verse about God's great love for the world, John 3. 16 (ESV); it is often included in the liturgy of our Holy Communion service:

> *'God so loved the world, that he gave his only Son, that whoever believes in him should not perish but have eternal life.'*

The story of Nicodemus is only recorded in St. John's gospel – perhaps he was the only one of the disciples who was not asleep at that late hour. Jesus told Nicodemus that no one could see the Kingdom of God unless he was born again.

What *is* love?

This time, we need to look at *love* as a noun. My dictionaries tell me that love is a strong feeling of affection or passion. Again, in school we may have learned that a noun, among other things, is a naming word. However, when we look more closely at this word as a noun, it still seems to cover a variety of meanings.

The love we feel for our marriage partners cannot possibly be the same feeling that we have when we love our children.

When we ask 'Do you love God?' we may want to know what kind of love it is that we have for God.

The way that we love God must be another, special kind of love that is quite different from the way we love our brothers and sisters.

If there are different types of love, what are they? .

Types of Love

As God is Love and He is eternal, Love is eternal. It goes right back to before the beginning of time as we know it on Planet Earth, before Creation and before God made Adam and Eve.

The different types of love seem to go a long way back in history, as they were revealed to us, too.

In the English language we really only have the one word for love. There are other words that we use, such as 'affection' and 'tenderness,' but if we want to distinguish between the different types of love we mostly need to describe what we mean by putting two or more words together in a phrase. In this way we might speak about 'romantic love,' 'brotherly love,' 'a mother's love for her children,' a father's love for his children,' 'children's love for their parents,' 'tough love', and best of all: 'our love of God' and 'God's love for us': Perfect love.

Words for Love in the Bible

The Old Testament

Most of the thirty-nine Books of the Old Testament Scriptures were originally written in what we now term Ancient Hebrew, but a few passages were in Aramaic,[78] a language that Jesus spoke. We have already looked briefly at the words for love in Ancient Hebrew.

The New Testament

In New Testament times, although Rome ruled much of the world, as it was known at that time, the language of the educated was Greek, so the twenty-seven Books of the New Testament were written in Greek, with a little Aramaic. The Aramaic language was still the common language of Judea in the time of Jesus and His Disciples, and in that language I understand that there are equivalents of the Greek *Eros, Philio/ Philos* and *Agape* that are found in the New Testament writings.

Greek words for love

The Greek language differentiates between four types of love much more neatly than we do in English. As we saw earlier (p. 20), the Greek language has four words for love, as it distinguishes between four different kinds of love. They are

- Eros
- Storge
- Philos
- Agape

---

[78] Genesis 31.47; Ezra 4.8 – 6.18; Jeremiah 10.11

DISCUSSION

1. How involved are we in our love for God?
2. When did you become aware that you were a Christian? Was it a surprising, serendipity, born again moment, or did it grow slowly in your understanding?
3. Do we ever fall asleep or let our minds wander when we know we should be praying – talking to our Father God?
4. Can it be helpful to look at love as a verb and then as a noun? Why?
5. What did you already know about the different kinds of love? Do you think they all come from God?

Prayer

Dear Father, you are our God of love. Help us to give ourselves to you each day afresh and use us, not as we choose, but according to your will for our lives. Teach us how to love you more and how to share your love with our neighbours. We pray in the precious name of Jesus. Amen.

CHAPTER ELEVEN

GREEK TYPES OF LOVE: A. EROS

In ancient Greek mythology Eros was the god of love. According to the story, he was the fourth god to appear when the world began. He is mentioned in Greek writings as far back as 700 BC. In early times he was a cult figure and later he evolved to be worshipped by a fertility cult.

When we look at illustrations from that time we find that Eros was always pictured as an adult in Greek mythology, but in Roman mythology the god of love was seen as a child called Cupid.

We are familiar with the names of both these ancient gods and we are aware that they have been adopted into the English language and culture. So we find a number of words in English that are connected with different areas of romantic and sexual love, such as *erotic, erotica, erotomania, erogenous* and even *cupidity,* which comes from a Latin word that means 'passionate desire.'

Eros as a Concept

The concept of *eros* that is usually accepted is that this

word represents the love between a man and a woman. It also suggests passionate physical desire, as we can see from the English words above that are derived from it. Psychologically speaking, *eros* is linked with self-preservation instincts as opposed to self-destruction instincts. Looked at from this viewpoint we can see that this notion seems to put the focus of *eros* on love being gratification for self, rather than on giving pleasure to another.

The Old Testament Notion

Previously we found that there were four Greek words for love. The first was *eros.* When we think about romantic, sexual love and the Bible, our thoughts probably go firstly to Adam and Eve and the concept that the love they shared must have been perfect before their temptation and The Fall. Then our thoughts probably go to the beautiful, provocative images evoked by the poetry of *The Song of Solomon*, also known as *The Song of Songs, which is Solomon's.*

However, the Old Testament was not written in Greek, but mostly in Hebrew. I have read that there are several Hebrew words that are translated into English as 'love,' but that they have subtly different meanings. The most frequent is *aheb*. This word was originally used to describe fertility cults in ancient civilizations and also the passionate love between a man and a woman. *Aheb* is found in the Bible over two hundred times. The first to use it in the Scriptures was Hosea, and instead of linking it with local fertility cults he linked it with marriage.

Eros and Christian Marriage

Eros, from a human vantage point, is a wonderful gift God has given to couples to celebrate their love of each other.

It's a delight for husband and wife to share this kind of love, not just for procreation, but also as an expression of joy in their union.

And how wonderful that can be, especially if that union is coupled with God, linked together with Him, when its expression is begun and ended in prayers of praise to our Heavenly Father for such a gift!

Eros and God

In The Old Testament, the Decalogue, the Ten Commandments,[79] puts God first as we have seen. If we examine them, we find that the majority of the Commandments are negative but those concerned with God and loving one's neighbour are positive.

When Jesus refused to worship Satan, He said,

> *'You shall worship the Lord your God and him only shall you serve.'*[80]

Is worship connected with loving God? If we are to obey the Commandments, then surely when we worship Him it must embrace adoring reverence and awe. We might see this as a problem, as it is a different kind of love from what we usually think of as being connected with *eros*.

Hosea used the Hebrew root, *aheb*, which was originally defined in a similar way to *eros*, but gave it a new meaning. *Aheb*, as we have seen, was used to describe pagan fertility cults, but Hosea extended and raised its meaning; in fact, it was completely and subtly changed so the word could be used to describe love and the One True God. By connecting the personal quality of *aheb* Hosea contributed to

---

[79] *See* Exodus Chapter 20
[80] Matthew 4.10 (ESV)

humanity's growing understanding of God's great love as He gradually revealed more and more facets of His character in the Old Testament Scriptures over a long period of time. Like *eros*, *aheb* is personal, spontaneous and intense, but it goes so much further as it is lifted to a much higher plane.

The intensity and joy of *eros* and *aheb* in human love help us to gain a greater understanding of how deeply God loves us. What a joy it can be when we accept His love and channel our delight into the intensity of our love and praise for Him.

Years ago I met a young woman about my age who was so beautiful I couldn't stop looking at her in awe. Sadly, although she wanted to marry, she never did, and I believe it was because she was such a perfectionist that she expected it in a mate as well. It's not that love is blind, as we're sometimes told, but because when we love we learn to be patient with our life-partner's faults. After all, I'm not so perfect myself, and yet my husband still loved me.

God's love is even more patient and accepting; He loves us, *just as we are*, warts and all. However, He doesn't love the sins we commit. God is so holy and pure, that of ourselves we cannot come close to Him, and are unable to have fellowship with Him, but He loves us when we accept Christ's great gift of love by sacrificing Himself so that our sins could be forgiven. Then we are made pure and can come close to our Father God who is so holy. That is what righteousness means, being made right with God.

What a wonderful gift that is!

DISCUSSION

1. Which of the Ten Commandments are negative and which are positive? Is it true that the ones concerned with God and loving our neighbour are all positive?
2. Do you think that the English words that are derived from *Eros* are related to the love between a man and a woman?
3. What do the Scriptures have to say about homosexuality?
4. In what ways can marital love and prayer be linked?
5. How can we achieve righteousness so that we can be in fellowship with God?

Prayer

Loving heavenly Father, you created us and gave us the joy and delight of human love and a way of explaining the intensity of our love for you. Give us strength through your Holy Spirit to use this beautiful gift in the way that you intended. Forgive us when we ignore its misuse in our community and help us, we pray, to live lives that are right with you. In Jesus' name we pray. Amen.

NOTES

CHAPTER TWELVE

GREEK TYPES OF LOVE: B. STORGE

The Greek word *storge* is pronounced 'stor-ge(t),' as in the word 'get' without the 't'. This word is not actually found in the Old Testament; as we have already discovered, the Old Testament was almost all written in Ancient Hebrew.

Parental Love

As we mentioned in passing earlier, the Greek language also has a separate word meaning the love of a parent for a child: *storge*. It is the love that is shared within a family. The love of parents for their children is another special kind of love; it is caring and protective, and probably also includes a little secret pride in their offspring, which assuredly includes grandparents' love for their grandchildren, too.

Our understanding of this type of love may be extended to include the love we share with others of the same culture, nationality or religion. It may also include the love of a sense of community.

Storge in the Old Testament

Although the word is not used in the Old Testament, there

are many examples there of this kind of love that was known and felt in primitive times as far back as the nineteenth century B.C. This is described in Genesis 44. 18 – 32. It tells of Jacob's love for his son Benjamin. When the missing cup that Joseph had hidden was found in Benjamin's sack, their eldest brother Judah spoke up although he risked punishment for doing so. He explained that Benjamin was a child of his father's old age and that Jacob loved him dearly. It's also interesting that Judah was the only full brother of Joseph; the others had a different mother.

Judah begged Joseph:

> *'He [Benjamin] alone is left of his mother' children, and his father loves him.'*[81]

Later in the conversation, he said,

> *'If he should leave his father, his father would die.'*[82]

In Leviticus, when the Lord God spoke to Moses and told him to speak to the people of Israel, telling them to be holy and set apart, it included the edict:

> *'You shall not take vengeance or bear a grudge against the sons of your own people.'* [83]

Storge in the New Testament

As the New Testament was written in Greek, we might expect to find the word here, but interestingly, the word is only used in the negative, and that occurs only twice,

---

[81] Genesis 44.20 (ESV)
[82] Genesis 44.22 (ESV)
[83] Leviticus 19. 18 (ESV)

written both times by St. Paul:

- In Romans 1.31, where he criticized the types of sinful, worldly people who knew that God existed but ignored Him and were filled with 'all manner of unrighteousness.' Paul lists these, including having ' no love.' I have heard that the word used in Greek was *astorgos*.

- This word appears again, in II Timothy 3.3 and this time it is translated into English as 'without love.' In verse one of this passage, Paul warns that a mark of the last days is that people will be devoid of natural love for their own families. Further, it is defined as 'devoid of natural or instinctive affection, without affection for kindred.'[84]

A New Testament example of parental love is the distraught synagogue leader who humbly knelt before Jesus begging Him to help his beloved daughter.[85]

The quote from Leviticus 19.18 (*See* above) has more, and this is repeated in Matthew 22.39. This repetition emphasizes the importance of love in the community, which is part of *storge*. In the King James Version it is translated as:

'Thou shalt love thy neighbour as thyself.'

There's another interesting word connected with *storge*, and again it was St. Paul who used it. It is a word that has been made by blending two words together, and I'd love to know if Paul had coined it. Those two words are *philos* (brotherly love, which we will look at in the next chapter),

---

[84] Information found at Biblia.com, using the ESV translation

[85] Matthew 9.18

and *storge*. Some people would call this a 'compound' word, but if we are being pedantic about it, it is really a 'blend,' or, to use the older word, a 'portmanteau,' as an 's' is missing in the middle and there is an addition at the end. It is *philostorgos*, although I have also seen it spelt *philostorgus*. It has a lovely meaning, as it is translated into English in Romans 12.10 in some translations as 'to cherish one's kindred.' It's a great word for Christians to ponder, as it can be extended to mean that, as part of the whole family of God's children around the world we love and cherish each other, or should do.

Although *storge* is not used by itself in the New Testament, or indeed in the whole of the Bible, there are many other references to the importance of love in both Testaments, beginning with the Lord God's words to Moses in Leviticus 19.18b (KJV):

> *'Thou shalt love thy neighbour as thyself;* ***I am*** *the Lord.'*

DISCUSSION

1. In the light of what we understand as storge, what should our attitude be to family violence?
2. What do you see as the difference between parents' *love* of their children and *doting* on them?
3. Compare real love for one's children with giving them everything they want. What can be the result of this?
4. We hear about sibling rivalry and read about it in the Bible. How can such rivalry result in bearing grudges? As parents, what can we do about it?
5. How can we show that we 'cherish our kindred' within our church family?

Prayer

Lord God, thank you that you are our Father in heaven and that you love us with the love of a parent. Forgive us when we go astray and bring us back to the warmth and protection of being your children. Help parents to control their frustration with their children and to recognize that their reactions can result in family violence. May love of their family overcome negative feelings as they turn to you and learn to exercise restrain through the guidance of your Holy Spirit. In Jesus' name, Amen.

NOTES

CHAPTER THIRTEEN

GREEK TYPES OF LOVE: C. PHILOS

Philos and Brotherly Love In the Old Testament

Again, as the Old Testament is mostly written in Hebrew, the word *philos or phileo* is not used, but the meaning of this Greek word is there. In fact, it has a number of different uses. We usually think of *phileo* as being brotherly love. This is seen as an inclusive term, as when the English word, 'man' is intended to embrace[86] 'woman.' Hence, we have sisterly love in this word, too.

This type of love also represents friendship, a love that is based on feelings, so it includes affection between human beings. There are many examples of this type of love in the Old Testament. The first that springs to mind is the lovely friendship of David and Jonathan.[87] There are many stories of friendships in the Old Testament, but a number of them ended in disaster. Among those that remained was the wonderful friendship between Abraham and God,[88] the adage in Proverbs 17.17 that a friend loves at all times, and in 18.24 we are told that to have a friend we need to be one, and also that a friend will stick closer than a brother. Then there is that lovely passage[89] that tells us that the beloved is more than a lover, he is also a friend.

---

[86] The ambiguity is intentional

[87] I Samuel 18.1

[88] II Chronicles 20.7 (ESV)

[89] Song of Solomon 5.16 (ESV)

In the New Testament

In the Greek of the New Testament we find both forms: *phileo* and *philea*. They express social love and affection between friends; it is a warm, tender kind of love. As it is based on feelings, God does not demand that we love like this; He gives us the choice. Although we may love in this way, we may not have consciously chosen it at all, it may just have happened. That is the best way: rather than striving for it, to simply allow it to come into our hearts.

Loving those of similar social and cultural groups is an important concept in the Bible. It is one of the wonderful ways we can show our love to each other, to those in our Church family, but then it extends out to our neighbours and to the world.

Philos is found over seventy times in the New Testament. A living language is continuously changing, and we find that as the meaning of *eros* extended, the meaning of *philos* also changed. Jesus is God's Son, and when we accept Him as Saviour we become children of God and can love Jesus as Friend and Brother as well as Saviour. What a privilege!

Looking at Philos Linguistically

English Words Using *philos* and *philea* as a Prefix

To diverge momentarily, there are several words in the English language that use the basic Greek *phileo* and *philea* as prefixes. Some, such as philadelphia, love between brothers and sisters, and philanthropia, love for humanity, showing others kindness, courtesy and thoughtfulness, can be found in the New Testament, but a living language always grows and changes, so there are more:

- philanthropist, a person who helps others, especially by donating money to a good cause; philanthropy, the practice of giving money to a worthy cause.
- philately, and its derivatives, such as philatelic and philatelist. As we know, the prefix means 'loving' and it has to do with stamp collecting, but the suffix is also interesting, as it comes from another Greek word which means exemption from payment, signifying that by using the postage stamp the recipient is exempt from paying, as sometimes happened before Roland Hill and his penny postage.
- philharmonic, means devoted to music.
- Other derivatives of words such as philology, the love and study of words, and philosophy, with the love of wisdom.
- There are even plants connected with loving: a mock orange with the name of *philadelphus*, loving one's brother, and *philodendron*, 'loving' and 'plant' or 'tree.'

Then there are other derivatives that present us with a more negative meaning: philander (v), (of a man) meaning to have numerous sexual relationships, and philanderer (n), a man who has many sexual relationships. There is a word for women with such tendencies as well, but it is not connected with *phileo*: *nymphomaniac*. This comes from both Greek and Roman mythology; the nymph was the spirit of nature, represented by a beautiful young woman.

English words using *philos* as a suffix

English words that use the Greek as a suffix end in *-phile.* These may also be positive, such as

- bibliophile, a fondness of books.
- Anglophile, a fondness of England; this suffix is added to many other countries, too.

Other words using the suffix *-phile* can also have a negative connotation, and this can cause difficulty, as we see in pedophile, a word which has changed over time from meaning 'one who has a fondness for children' (which most of us would claim to be) into something far more morbid (which we most certainly would not want to be!).

Philos Love - in the Bible, and Now

Our interest in linguistics has caused a divergence, so to return to *philos/ philea* in the Bible, we find that, although the actual words used in the Old Testament may not be the Greek of the New Testament, the meaning is there.

As we have seen, the intensity of *eros* helps us understand the intensity of our love for God. *Storge* and p*hilos* are types of love that helps us to deepen our feelings of this great gift of love that He has bestowed on us; they bring the kind of love that is caring, love that shares warmth and friendship.

DISCUSSION

1. Do you take your brothers and sisters for granted, or do you work at having a loving relationship with them?
2. Are brotherly/sisterly love and the love of a friend the same? Which is more important to you?
3. What would your ideal friend be like? Would you be the same for that person?
4. Do you maintain friendships with others with the same social and cultural backgrounds as yourself? How do you do that?
5. Is it important to build and maintain friendly relationships with people of cultures that are different from your own? How do you do that?

Prayer

Praise you Lord for our brothers and sisters and our good friends. What a blessing they are to us! May we also be a blessing to them. Help us to learn about other social and cultural groups from our own, to overcome the differences and show your love in the friendships that we work on to build and maintain within our church family and in the community where we live. We pray in the name of our Friend and Saviour, Jesus Christ.

Amen

NOTES

CHAPTER FOURTEEN

GREEK TYPES OF LOVE: D. AGAPE

Keeping the Best Until Last

In examining the different Greek words for our English word of 'love,' we have looked at *eros*, *storge* and *philos* in the Bible, but we've saved the best until last: *agap*e love. This is the highest possible form of love; it is altruistic love, that is, it is the kind of love that shows thoughtfulness for the needs and wellbeing of other people; it is an unselfish concern for others and the purest kind of love there can be. Perhaps we can see in *agape* love something of the other three loves, especially the gently, caring, protective love that we see in *storge*; this is God's unconditional love for His people and our love for Him.

The Old Testament

If we go back to the Scriptures of the Old Testament and the time of Moses, we can learn much about how to live and love from the Ten Commandments[90] that

[90] Exodus 20.3 - 17

God gave His people, the Children of Israel, as they wandered in the desert. In them we find that God shows

> *'steadfast love to the thousandth generation of those who love me and keep my commandments.'*[91]

There were many other rules that expanded on these in several of the Old Testament Books after that, too.

The first of the Ten Commandments[92] concern how God's people are to live before Him, while the later ones are connected with rules on how His people are to live with each other.[93]

The New Testament

In the New Testament we find just one commandment from Jesus and that sums up all those that have gone before in one brief sentence:

> *'A new commandment I give to you, that you love one another: just as I have loved you, you also are to love one another.'*[94]

What wonderful love that is! Jesus loves us so much that He gave HIs life for us and for all humanity in order that we could be forgiven and made holy. Only when we accept this gift can we come close to our Heavenly Father who is so pure, and have fellowship with Him. When we believe in Jesus Christ and live that commandment, we can have abundant life here on earth and when we die we will have everlasting life and be with our glorious Father for eternity.

---

[91] Exodus 20.6 (NRSV)
[92] Exodus 20.3 - 11
[93] Exodus 20.11-17
[94] John 13.34 (ESV)

Word-building Time

This time, I have been unable to find other words that are built on the word *agape*. It stands alone, as it is so special, so profound. However, the word itself can have other meanings:

Firstly, with a different pronunciation, it is agape (of course, the taxonomy is different, but the spelling in English is the same):

- having the mouth wide open in astonishment
- wide open, like a gate

Secondly, and this is the one that we are concerned with; here it is pronounced 'agapé' and it has two meanings:

- What we have described as altruistic love
- A meal the early Christians shared in fellowship together

This kind of love is the Greek *agape* and the wonder of it can leave us with mouths wide open, *agape*, in astonishment!

Jesus and Peter

Remember that puzzling occasion when Jesus asked Peter three times,

'Do you love me?'[95]

Have you ever wondered why Jesus asked Peter that question three times?[96] Well, that is our English translation.

---

[95] John 21.15 - 17

[96] In linguistics this is an oratory stylistic technique known as ternary repetition

Apparently two different words were used here in the original Greek: Twice Jesus asked Peter using *agape*, but Peter found this difficult to answer, and used *phileo* in his response; he loved Jesus as a brother. The third time Jesus used *phileo* and this time Peter was able to answer this happily: Yes, he loved Jesus as a brother. Jesus was possibly teaching Peter about *agape* love, as being unconditional love. Asking the question three times may also have had another purpose, as Peter was feeling so downhearted at having denied Jesus three times, and this could have helped him to feel forgiven and released, so regaining his freedom in Jesus.

The Highest Kind of Love in the Bible

Agape describes Divine love, the highest and purest kind of love we can ever find is right there in the Bible. It is unconditional, mature love and when we love like that we take pleasure in replacing undesirable characteristics in our lives - like selfishness, pride and love of our possessions - with unselfishness, humility, generosity and with putting others and their needs first before our own.

The quoted commandment of Jesus is from St. John's Gospel.[97] John is often known as 'the Apostle of love' as he wrote so much about it. In his three Letters that have been preserved for us in the New Testament there is even more about *agape* love, especially in 1 John:

- As God loves us, so we should love Him and one another.
- Our *agape* love is evidence of our love of God - Father, Son and Holy Spirit.

We learn from St. John that love, without action, is of little

[97] John 13.34

value. As Christians, our *agape* love must be seen in the way we live our lives and how we share that love with others. When we obey God's law of love by doing this, His Holy Spirit will come into our hearts and we will grow to become more like Jesus. May we, as Christians, obey that law, totally relying on God's enabling grace, so that His love in us is apparent in our truth, sincerity, humility and holiness.

Do you love God?

We can't see God, so how can we love someone we can't see? Paul tells us in his *First Letter to Corinthians* that loving God is the greatest thing we can ever do. Yes, it's an emotion, but one that we choose through our will.

How do we express our love for God? By obeying His Word, worshipping and thanking Him, and by loving other people and sharing God's love with them.

For us, as sinful humans, *agape* love, like *eros, storge* and *phileo*, can also be a problem. We know the ideal we strive for, but it is another matter achieving this, and especially in keeping our footsteps following the right pathway.

In Chapter Seventeen we will look at C. S. Lewis' book, '*The Four Loves*' as he suggests solutions.

DISCUSSION

1. Why is *agape* the best kind of love?
2. What are the two conditions in the Ten Commandments that God placed on our being blessed as recipients of His love?
3. Explain the reward that is available for us if we obey Jesus' commandment in John 13.34.
4. What is the greatest thing we can ever do? How can we achieve it?
5. List some of the ways in which we can express our love for God.

Prayer

All-loving Father in heaven, sometimes we find it difficult to love you as we should. Help us to better love you and the people you have created wherever they may be. Grant that we may learn how to love you when there is no light to show us that you are here with us. Hold us tight in the embrace of your love so that we may spread its warmth to others. In the name of your Son, Jesus. Amen.

CHAPTER FIFTEEN

UNPACKING THE QUESTION

3. YOU

Do you love God?

That question is for me! Personally. Do ***I*** love God? Well, yes, I do, but how much do I love Him? The Ten Commandments God gave to the Children of Israel and that we read about in Exodus 20. 2-17 are quite clear. A little further on in the Old Testament, in Deuteronomy, Moses elaborates on the First Commandment:

> *'You shall love the Lord your God with all your heart, and with all your soul, and with all your might. Keep these words... in your heart. Recite them to your children and talk about them ... at home and when you are away, when you lie down and when you rise...write them on the doorposts.'*[98]

Remember how, thousands of years later, Jesus condensed these Ten Commandments into just two:

[98] Deuteronomy 6.5 – 9 (NRSV)

> *'You shall love the Lord your God with all your heart, and with all your soul and with all your mind and with all your strength.' The second is this: 'You shall love your neighbour as yourself.' There is no other commandment greater than these.'*[99]

With all my heart, soul, mind and strength? That's everything that I'm capable of, and then some; absolutely the whole of me. Am I capable of loving like that? Especially when it concerns my love for God. Sometimes I get so wrapped up in what I'm doing, or my latest project, that I may forget all about Him for the whole day until it comes to my prayer time at night. It would be impossible for me in my own strength. This is where the great infilling of the Holy Spirit comes in; it is only in His power that I can live in love with God.

If I try to obey these two commandments of Jesus, and live my life by them, there is no need for the rest of the Ten Commandments, because I will be obeying them anyway. Is it that easy? Those Children of Israel, who wandered in the desert for forty years after escaping from Egypt, did not find them easy at all! They were always being punished for breaking them. How will I fare if I disobey?

When we looked at those Ten Commandments before, we discovered that while the ones about God are positive, there are others that are negative, warnings of the things that we should not do.

---

[99] Mark 12.30 – 31 (ESV)

Action and Inaction

Later Jesus said that we do not only break the commandments by our actions, but also by our thoughts and inaction. There are sins of omission as well as of commission.

The things we do and should not, the sins of commission, are often glaringly obvious to ourselves and even to others. We see them as the 'You shall not' Commandments, and look at them as the big ones. The sins of omission are not always so obvious, and so we look at them as more minor sins, but when we neglect to do things that we should do, God knows – and so do we. Did we skip our Quiet Time yesterday morning? Did we pass by newcomers to our church community, and not welcome them? There are so many little things that we should do, but omit, while trying to convince ourselves that they're such small things and so quite unimportant, but these are sins against God in His sight. Showing our love for God and being obedient to Him in the way we live is vital for our spiritual wellbeing – and our relationship with Him.

Are there barriers to my loving and obeying God? What causes those barriers?

What prevents me from loving?

As we noticed before, the word 'love' in this question is a verb; it is what we actively *do*. Loving is also an emotion, a feeling, and it's a positive one. So often in our lives we can find ourselves held back from showing our love, as we would like to do, by negative emotions. The use in our question of 'You' really means 'Me' as the question was directed to me, but it's also relevant for each of us.

So often our lives are swayed by negative as well as positive emotions, aren't they? In our hearts we know the right direction to go, following God's path, but Satan is alive and well and we can feel him pulling us in quite the opposite direction. We can even imagine that the wrong thing we have done is someone else's fault anyway. Remember the words of that old song:

'When I point my finger at my neighbour, three more are pointing back at me'?

Negative Emotions

Sometimes small things cause negative responses and emotions in our lives and then, if we do not stay alert and careful, they can build up until they take over all our thoughts and actions.

Anger: You're driving along, obeying all the road rules and suddenly someone cuts in and you have to brake suddenly, causing discomfort to your passengers. All thoughts of love vanish. You want to vent your anger and get back at that other driver. I know; I've been there! Anger keeps love at bay. We fear that if our love grows there may be too much emotion, so we hold onto our negative feelings.

A Grudge: Holding a grudge takes time and energy. Someone wrongs us and we refuse to forgive. We hold that grudge until we're not sure what we'd do without it. It lingers and builds if we don't deal with it. Keeping a grasp of it can hurt us more than the person who wronged us.

Personal Betrayal: We often replay personal betrayal and hurt and we find that moving on is difficult. I remember my first teaching appointment, which I had prayed for, as it was in a Children's Home and I wanted to help those small outcasts of society. Soon I loved those children and cared deeply as I watched their young lives develop, and then one of 'my' children was adopted. I should have been glad, but I was hurt; I missed the interaction with this intelligent child. A similar thing can happen with friendships: we share personal experiences with a friend or acquaintance and then find that the confidence was passed on – gossip can be a great destroyer of personal relationships.

Resentment: Some event occurs or someone says something we think is an insult and we feel resentful. If we harbour that resentment it may stop us from being hurt again, as we place ourselves at a distance from that person, but this attitude will not help us to build loving relationships and it is we, ourselves, who will suffer.

Not Forgiving: Years ago I was struck by Corrie ten Boom's[100] remarks that we may think we have forgiven someone, but then keep a relevant letter, just in case we need it as proof; and when we think about it we realize

---

[100] **Cornelia "Corrie" ten Boom** (15 April 1892 – 15 April 1983) was a Dutch Christian who, with her father and family, helped many Jews escape the Nazi Holocaust during World War II. She was imprisoned for her actions. Her most famous book, *The Hiding Place*, describes the ordeal.

that we haven't really forgiven. Remember the Lord's Prayer: we ask God to forgive us

*'**as** we forgive those who sin against us.'*

To have God's forgiveness, *we* must forgive. We need to release that anger, grudge, or feeling of betrayal and resentment; it is holding us back. When we concentrate on negative emotions they pull us down and right away from loving God and our neighbour.

Positive Emotions

We need to keep our emotions positive and to love the Lord our God so we can grow a future where we can nurture new, healthy ideas. Once we shake off the shackles that hold us back we can move on and start to heal, to love and be loved, but we can only do that in the power of the Holy Spirit.

God is more interested in the way we travel on life's journey than in our career, our earthly wealth and our achievements. When we start to think positively, we become so much healthier in both our bodies and spiritually. This can also have an effect on those around us.

How much lovelier it is to be positive and affirming in our emotions and attitudes towards others! And how it can help us in our relationships with God, our family and our friends and neighbours!

DISCUSSION

1. *'You shall love the Lord your God with all your heart, and with all your soul, and with all your might'* (Deut. 6.5, NRSV). Do we keep this commandment, recite and talk about it with our children – and write it on our doorpost? Is it visible in the way we live"
2. This chapter is all about me - and my own personal response to God's love. In what ways am I active or inactive in the way I show my love for Him?
3. What is my response to the temptations that Satan puts in my way?
4. How can we free ourselves from sluggishness and self-complacency?
5. Meditate on the wonder that God can release us from negativity and praise Him for the joy that comes when we allow His love to fill our hearts through the power of the Holy Spirit.

Prayer

Father, forgive me for the times when I am self-centred and think only of myself and my needs. Help me to rise above such things, to be strong in the power of the Holy Spirit and to say those words: 'Get thee behind me, Satan.' Praise you, Father, for your abiding love and fill me with joy and enthusiasm so that I may live as you would have me do. Through Jesus Christ, my Lord. Amen.

NOTES

CHAPTER SIXTEEN

UNPACKING THE QUESTION

4. DO

The *Doing* of Loving God

Once I understand how and when to use the different types of love, it's my doing, my actions, which are important. We know where that road that is paved with good intentions leads; I don't want to go there. In James (2.22a, KJV) we read,

'Be ye doers of the word, and not hearers only.'

This verse goes on to tell us that if we are hearers only, we deceive ourselves. In other words, if we go to church regularly and live 'good' lives, but do not put our Christianity into action, we're not really Christians at all. Strong words!

Christian love is about serving and sharing our love. I once read that, 'you cannot serve from an empty vessel.' How true! We need to be filled with God's love before we can love Him and love others, and show that love in the way we serve. The Bible is our guidebook: it contains the world's greatest love story, as it tells us about the infinite love of God for His people. Remember that saying of D. L. Moody:

'Either this book will keep you from sin or sin will keep you from this book.'

That is so true! The choice is ours, but lip service is not enough; we need to do something about it as well.

To **DO** requires action on our part: we are to love God and our neighbour. My neighbour is anyone who needs help, whether close at hand or on the other side of the world. We're even told to love our enemies, but we do not love the bad things that people (or we) do. After all, God still loves us and we're not exactly perfect! 'Love the sinner, not the sin,' is a good slogan, even, or perhaps especially within families and our church family. If we love God, we need to put that *agape* love into action. We must show it in our lives by the way we live, in the way we love our neighbours, in the way we thank God for His wonderful love, in the way we read His word and have fellowship with Him and with each other, and in the way that we praise Him for all that He *is*. We need to discover our God-given gifts and talents and use them wisely. I remember speaking to a group of Mothers Union Karen refugees, Burmese Christians, and we see these words below:

YOUR GIFT? DISCOVER AND CELEBRATE
နတၢ်လၣ်မ့ၢ်မနုၤလဲၣ်. ယုကွၢ်ထံၣ်ဒီးသ့ၣ်ညါအီၤလီၤတံၢ်လီၤဆဲးတက့ၢ်.

Recently, in my daily Quiet Time readings, I found a devotional by J. I. Packer. Entitled 'The Greatest Thing,'[101] it was based on that much loved thirteenth chapter of Paul's first *Letter to the Corinthians*. Packer wrote that the word *agape* appeared to be a Christian invention, that it had been practically non-existent before New Testament times, coming from the advent of Jesus Christ. Perhaps that's why it confused Peter so much. Packer suggests that *Agape* was a supernatural fruit of the Spirit[102] that Paul wrote about.

---

[101] J. I. Packer, in Blaiklock and Packer, 1974, Bible Characters and Doctrines Volume 11: 15. London: Scripture Union, p. 28

[102] Galatians 5.22 - 23

He felt that it was to do with the will rather than an emotion, as Christians are commanded to love their enemies and people that they do not like. He writes that to do this is the greatest thing in the world and through it we can become more like Christ.

Packer then discusses what he sees as Paul's three 'Ps' of love: its primacy, profile and permanence in relation to the Corinthians, and these can be applicable to us, too. So many centuries later much in our way of life has changed, but not love, because God is love and God does not change.

1. ***The Primacy of Love***: The people of the Corinthian churches were so concerned with many things relating to their Christian living. Packer points out that Paul's 'tongues, prophetic gifts, theological expertise and miracle-working faith'[103] were all gifts from God. These attributes, so important in the early church are still important today, yet Christians in many places continue to find they have lost all their worldly possessions or that they are martyred for their faith. Love is not there. Paul points out that, for the Christian, love is so much more important than many other things in our lives that all else fades before it. The Christian may be very gifted with any number of abilities and use these gifts to work tirelessly for others, but if there is no love, all this activity is pointless. The good works will vanish away and become valueless and the person of no account in God's kingdom, unless everything is done in His love.

2. ***The Profile of Love***: This beautiful passage is often read at weddings, but this kind of love is so

[103] To be found in I Corinthians 13

much more. Packer[104] suggests that these statements Paul makes about love actually combine to make up a portrait of Jesus. It is His profile: Jesus is God's Son, part of God Himself, and God is love. If we understand this, we know so much more of our Saviour. Paul's assessment of the Corinthians, that they were 'bumptious, contentious, suspicious, presumptuous, arrogant, self-assertive, critical, irresponsible in spirit' caused him to call them 'carnal, and spiritually babyish.'[105] This list of the Corinthians' undesirable attributes reminds me of those Paul enumerated in his *Letter to the Galatians.*[106] Love does not condone these sins of other people, as we are likely to be guilty of them ourselves. Instead, we should concentrate on showing our love by our actions and helping ourselves and others to overcome these traits.

3. ***The Permanence of Love***: As in Galatians, where Paul goes on to list the antidote for these undesirable attributes, that is, the Fruit[107] that God gives us through the power of the Holy Spirit; the most important part of love is its permanence. It seems to me that *agape* is the most important type of love. When we recognize and accept God's love into our lives and show it in the way that we live, even when we die and everything else of our earthly lives has passed away, this love will remain for us into eternity. So, again, as Paul wrote in his Letter to the Galatians,

[104]Packer, p. 28
[105] ibid
[106] Galatians 5.19 - 21
[107] ibid 5.22 - 23

'If we live in the Spirit, let us also keep in step with the Spirit.'[108]

On this journey of life we have been given free choice, pray that we make the right choice, love God and our neighbour and show this in our actions and what we DO, as we keep our walk on the onward and upward way.

DISCUSSION

1. How can we be doers and not hearers only:
    a. As an individual?
    b. As a group?
2. How can we discover our God-given gifts? Should we celebrate them or just use them?
3. Why would Packer refer to *agape* as a 'supernatural' gift? What did he mean?
4. In 1 Corinthians 13 Paul wrote about love as he saw it expressed in Jesus Christ. What can we learn from this about the way we should live the Christian life?
5. What does Packer mean by the 'permanence of love'?

---

[108] Galatians 5.25

Prayer

Father, praise you for the wonderful gifts that you have given us. Please help us to grow these gifts and use them to your glory. May we be your people of action who follow the example of your Son Jesus so that we may not be just hearers of your Word, but doers to the utmost of our abilities. We ask this in the name of Jesus who loved us so much that he gave his life for us. Amen.

CHAPTER SEVENTEEN

GIFT-LOVE AND NEED-LOVE

When we looked into each type of love, we may have found that we are very vulnerable and there are hurdles and pitfalls that hamper and may even entrap us on our walk. Each kind of love we have learned about appears to reveal that it is composed of both positives and negatives and the pathway can seem just too hard to follow.

However, in his book, '*The Four Loves,*' C. S. Lewis proposes that each of the four Greek types of love can be seen from the viewpoint of 'gift-love' and 'need-love.' He does not use the Greek names, but instead provides an English language equivalent for each, such as erotic love, brotherly love and charity. He believes that the highest type of love cannot stand without the lowest, meaning that in order to understand the highest love, what we have referred to as *agape*, we need to be able to contrast it with the lowest form. He suggests that each type of love can be seen as both Gift-love and Need-love, and he warns that while one type of love can be the highest, it can also become the lowest if we do not beware.

Gift-love

Gift-love is when we give our love as a gift; it is like the Dobuan '*oboboma*'[109] that I wrote about earlier. It is love that is given freely, without any expectation of a gift of that type of love in return; it implies that the recipient needs to choose to accept the gift that is offered. We still have that power of choice.

At its highest, Lewis relates this kind of love to Divine love, where the Father gives all to His Son; the Son gives Himself to God and to the world and He gives the world to the Father. Because God is love, Gift-loves are God-like and when we give this kind of love, not expecting anything in return, it brings us closer to God and helps us to become more like Him. However, so often we may feel that if we give love in this way we need some kind of reciprocation.

Need-love

Need-love is best seen in situations where we realize that there is a need for love, such as a child needing love from a parent, but this is also true of a parent, who needs to love the child, too. Lewis points out that it is not good for people to be alone, they need love; he suggests that if we prefer to be always alone we are not living a healthy life spiritually. Spiritual health reaches its peak when we admit our need-love for God and ask Him for His Gift-love, needing to love Him in return. However, Need-love between people may cause us to be greedy and press for more love than the other people are ready or able to give.

---

[109] *See* p. 20

What is Love?

Love in this context is not love unless it is God-like and Gift-love. If we apply Need-love to, for example, erotic love, we may allow the need to overtake our gift of the love. By doing this, we prevent it from being true love, and it can decline into becoming a god, so in the end it is not true love at all.

We need to know that our love is built on a firm foundation so that it can rise to a higher plane without coming crashing down. Falling in love with someone is not the same type of love as loving God, which can help to purify us and lead us to live holier lives.

Lesser Kinds of Love

Likes: At the other end of the continuum, but related to our loves, are our 'likes.' These include things that unexpectedly give us pleasure, such as the lovely perfume of flowers that we suddenly and unexpectedly catch. We also need things like this in our lives, and Lewis terms these 'Need-pleasure' and 'Pleasure-appreciation.'

- **Need-Pleasure**: We all need pleasure in our lives, but if we seek after it, Need-pleasure can lead to wrongful desire: lust and covetousness. Once satisfied, the pleasure received can vanish away and be quickly forgotten.

- **Pleasure-appreciation**: When we see something lovely that occurs unexpectedly, such as

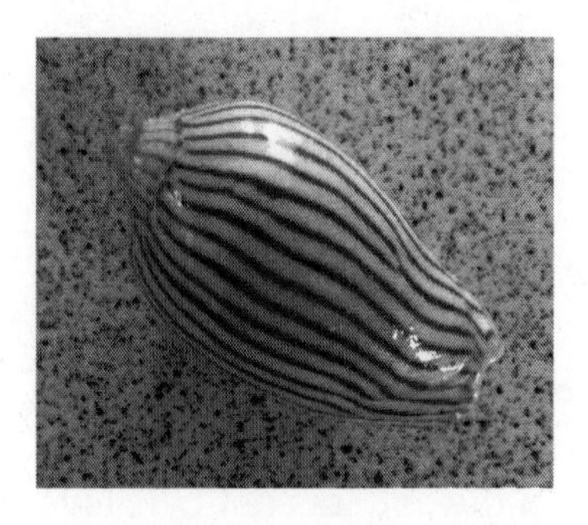

a beautiful sunset, or the beautiful markings on a sea-shell, it can give great Pleasure-appreciation that may be remembered for many years. God's love is like that. We may suddenly experience it, and our Pleasure-appreciation may continue right through this life and into eternity.

Affection: Lewis relates affection to the Greek *storge*; it is the love of children for their parents. This may be Need-love, while affection of parents for their children is seen as Gift-love. However, these can be reversed, for example, a mother's affection for her child may be Need-love. Where affection is mutual it can become humble and homely; it does not expect too much and it mixes with the other loves because it is familiar, but it also broadens our minds and teaches us to appreciate others. As affection includes both Need-love and Gift-love it can become ambivalent and produce happiness only if commonsense is added. If we try to live by affection alone, it can take over and become a god that we worship and then it turns into a demon.

Friendship: Often friendship is not considered a love at all. Without sexual love (*eros*) we would not have been begotten and without affection (*storge*) we would not have been reared, but if our circumstances demand it we can live without friendship or companionship. Friendship is the least jealous of the loves. Love is face to face; friendship is side by side.

Friendship must be based on something, such as a shared interest and it is at its best when it is between a man and a man or a woman and a woman. It is Appreciative love and is different from the love between a person and God. Lewis warns that if friendship is between different sexes, it is likely to become erotic love.

C.S Lewis has some helpful things to say that can extend our understanding of what love is and how to address some of the problems that may arise as we think more deeply about this wonderful gift from our Heavenly Father.

DISCUSSION

1. C. S. Lewis has condensed the four Greek loves to only two: Gift-love and Need-love. Do you think this is helpful to our understanding of the qualities of the different kinds of love? Why?
2. What does the word 'charity' mean in this context?
3. What are the problems that can arise if we concentrate in our lives on Need-love?
4. What are some of the difficulties that can be caused by affection?
5. Do you agree that true friendship can only be between a man and a man or a woman and a woman? Does this mean that there is really no such thing as altruistic love (the seeking the welfare of others rather than of self)?

Prayer

God of love, we have been learning that there are so many different ways of loving. Through your Holy Spirit teach us the right pathway to follow in our loving so that we may choose wisely and love in ways that are according to your will. Praise you for the wonderful, pure gift of your love. May we love you now and always, right into eternity. In the name of Jesus, Messiah and Saviour. Amen.

CHAPTER EIGHTEEN

CONCLUSION

Do you love God?

However imperfectly we love God, the answer is surely a resounding YES!

We have reached the end of a long answer to a short but very deep question. Thankfully, there is never a conclusion to God's love for us; may there never be a conclusion to our love for Him. We learned that God has gradually revealed Himself and His character to His people through the ages covered in the Bible, and since those times. Now we are ready for Him to be revealed to our hearts so that we can grow in our love and understanding of Him.

It's not healthy to be for ever inward looking, but sometimes it is good to stand back and look objectively at ourselves and scrutinize the way we have chosen to live. We don't always understand and accept that our God is so great, yet He calls us His precious children, and freely gives us His love.

God's love is a gift and it's there for us to take; there is no need to strive after it. All we need to do is open our hearts and accept it, fill our hearts with it and talk to Him, our Heavenly Father, and thank Him, through Jesus. Then His Holy Spirit will teach us how to love God in a way that is acceptable to Him.

If we are to live the Christian life, it is imperative that we show our love in the way that we share that love with our neighbours. Then God's love can be seen in our lives through the way we live and cultivate the 'Fruit of the Spirit.' Whether we use that fruit, whether we act or not is our choice. May we use that gift of love wisely.

To mix our metaphors, we may go to church regularly and appear to be good, clean-living Christians, but then continue in Need-love as babes that perpetually need feeding with milk, rather than fully accepting – and giving - God's Gift-love which leads us on to the meat that feeds Christian maturity.

On the other hand, we may have turned back from the time when we learned about God's love in giving His Son and the time when we accepted Christ's sacrifice on the cross for the forgiveness of our sins. Through our repentance, God forgave our sins and we were made clean to live our lives in keeping with His commandments. When we are made clean we become holy so that we can approach our God Who is so holy, and have wonderful fellowship with Him. If we turn back from that path we wander off and separate ourselves from God. Then we lose touch with the reality of what the Christian life is about. We may still call ourselves Christians, but we have become unproductive Christians.

When we think about *how* we love God, let us remind ourselves again of those commandments that were first given by God, that are still repeated twice a day by faithful Jews, and then condensed to their very essence by Jesus:

> *'You shall love the Lord your God with all your heart and with all your soul and with all your mind and with all your strength.' The second is this: 'You shall*

> *love your neighbour as yourself.' There is no other commandment greater than these.'*[110]

Put simply, we love God because He first loved us and the way we can love Him is to just tell Him! Then we need to prove it by showing it in the way that we live.

When we allow the lure of the world to draw us back from obeying Jesus' two great commandments, our steps along the path on our journey of life will quickly descend to the mud and slush of the valleys. It is my prayer that if you and I both continue to obey these commandments of Jesus and try to live a godly life, even when we stumble, as we surely will, God's Spirit will lift us up and place our feet back on the right way as we progress towards the heights, assured of the final reward of glorious eternal life at the end of our earth journey.

[110] Mark 12.28 – 31 (ESV)

Finally, if you can commit yourself wholeheartedly to our great Creator God, pray with me this beautiful prayer written by a French hermit. He was assassinated in the Sahara in 1916. In 1959 the French Government issued a stamp in his honour.

A Prayer of Charles de Foucauld

Father, I abandon myself into your hands.
Do with me what you will,
Whatever You do I will thank You.
I am ready for all; I accept all.
Let only Your will be done in me,
As in all Your creatures,
And I will ask nothing else, my Lord.

Into your hands I commend my spirit,
I give it to You with all the love of my heart,
For I love You, Lord, and so need to give myself,
To surrender myself into Your hands
With a trust beyond all measure,
Because You are my Father. Amen.

BIBLIOGRAPHY

BOOKS

Blaiklock, E.M. and J. I. Packer, 1974. Bible Characters and Doctrines. London: Scripture Union.

Cranfield, C.E.B. 1957. In Richardson, Alan, ed. 1957. A Theological Word Book of the Bible. Great Britain: S.C.M. Press.

Jacobus, Melancthon W., Edward E. Nourse and Andrew C. Zenos, eds. 1926. A New Standard Bible Dictionary: Designed as a comprehensive help to the study of the Scriptures, their languages, literary problems, history, biography, manners and customs, and their religious teachings. New York and London: Funk & Wagnalls.

Lewis, C. S. 1960. The Four Loves. London: Harper Collins.

Packer, J. I. 1974. Doctrinal Studies: Life in Christ, Volume 11: 15: 'The Greatest Thing' in Blaiklock and Packer, Bible Characters and Doctrines. London: Scripture Union.

Packer, J. I., Wayne Grudem and Ajith Fernando, eds. 2012. Global Study Bible: English Standard Version. Wheaton, Illinois: Crossway.

Richardson, Alan, ed. 1957. A Theological Word Book of the Bible. Great Britain: S.C.M. Press.

Scott-Branagan, Bronwen J. 2014. St. Paul's Letter to the Celts. Melbourne, Australia: BSB Ventures.

Strong, James, 2007. Strong's Exhaustive Concordance of the Bible. Updated and expanded edition. Peabody, Massachusetts: Hendrickson.

ELECTRONIC REFERENCES

http://en.wikipedia.org/wiki/Corrie_ten_Boom

http://en.wikipedia.org/wiki/Jacob_Astley,_1st_Baron_Astley_of_Reading

http://typesoflove.org/the-three-types-of-love-in-the-bible

BOOKS BY BRONWEN SCOTT-BRANAGAN

BIBLE STUDY BOOKS

ST. PAUL'S LETTER TO THE CELTS

ISBN: 9780980282788

Paperback 216 pages

$17.50

Galatia was home for three Celtic tribes. This book looks at Paul's *Letter to the Galatians* and its continuing relevance for Celts and all who read it today. It includes questions for personal or group study.

A LENTEN JOURNEY: PAUL'S LETTER TO THE EPHESIANS

ISBN: 9780980282719

Paperback 76 pages

$14.95

A series of six small group studies examine *The Letter of Paul to the Ephesians.* It includes questions for discussion and activities for home; each study is intended to have a duration of about an hour.

HOLY BIBLE HELPMATE

ISBN: 9780980282733

Paperback 100 pages

$14.00

A brief overview of each Book of the Bible is followed by a three-year Lectionary, themes for Sundays and special days, a Glossary and a useful list of Bible texts on a variety of topics that are useful for study or preaching. Written for pastors in the PNG Islands and profit goes to reducing the cost for these pastors.

BIOGRAPHY

THE MEMOIRS OF GENEVIEVE CUTLER

ISBN: 9780992599638

Paperback 258 pages Includes many photographs

$25.00

Meet Genevieve, born into a Christian family in Brighton, Melbourne, worked on *The Argus*; World War II creator of The BLOTS, then Company Officer; trained as a nurse at The Alfred; spent eighteen years in Africa as Bishop Stanway's secretary, nursing sister with CMS, then Save the Children; writer who espoused many causes. Her life of faith, dedication and service is a great example.

CHILDREN'S BOOKS

AGES 3-6

Picture Story Book

CHIPS QUACKETY

ISBN: 9781612047195

32 colour illustrations by the author; 36 pages $15.95

At the Queen Victoria Market in Melbourne, Elly persuades her parents to buy a tiny duckling. He is named Chips Quackety and the family has a number of adventures as Elly and her parents learn to care for the little duckling and keep it happy as it grows. The story is based on a real family happening.

AGES 4-8

Picture Story Book

THE PANDANUS PEOPLE

ISBN: 978608600069 10 colour illustrations by the author Paperback 29 pages $13.75

Billy and Jilly live in a pandanus tree and have some amazing adventures, learn to listen to instructions, be nice to others and obey family rules. The gentle Christian undertone helps children connect faith to their everyday behaviour.

AGES 5-9

Picture Story Book

CHRISTMAS SNOW

ISBN: 9780992599621
Paperback Illustrated by the author 40 pages
$25.00

Awarded First Prize in Macmillan Publishing Company's competition for teachers. The story is of a young PNG Island lad's adventures with teachers and classmates as they visit a mountain village to sing carols on Christmas Eve, just before midnight.

AGES 8-12

The Joan Murray Series: 1

JOAN AND THE GREAT DEPRESSION

ISBN: 978098028257 Paperback 137 pages
$13.75

Joan, who lives in Black Rock, Melbourne, experiences The Great Depression of the early 1930s. It is a time of adventure with friends as she is learning to trust in God and cope with the many changes that occur in her life.

AGES 8-12

The Joan Murray Series: 2

JOAN: SUNSHINE AND SHADOWS

ISBN: 9780992599614 Paperback 188 pages $15.50

Joan's 1930s adventures continue as the Great Depression is fading, but the possibility of war casts a shadow over the lives of many people. Joan and her family live in Black Rock, with special fun times away at the family's holiday house in Rosebud on the Mornington Peninsula.

THE GREAT WAR

DAD, THE GREAT WAR AND BEYOND

Ebook Available from Amazon
46 pages contains illustrations and text $3.99

POETRY

DITHYRAMBLES: POEMS OF THE HEART

ISBN: 978098028276

Paperback 96 pages

Black and white illustrations $15.95

Bronwen's poems from childhood until the present day. Some are humorous, some serious for special occasions, and some have a Christian context. The title is based on the word dithyrambic: 'wildly enthusiastic and irregular.'

FAMILY

CORNISH KINSFOLK: FROM CORNWALL TO CASTLEMAINE

ISBN: 9780980282702

Paperback 406 pages
$35.00

This Family tree book was awarded First Prize in Castlemaine Historical Society Awards, 2006. Comments include: 'Sets high standard…very well written and presented.' It includes Bibliography and comprehensive index.

THIS IS OUR STORY

ISBN: 9780980282771 Paperback 220 pages

Includes photographs $14.95

This book covers our years as missionary teachers with our family on Fergusson Island in the D'Entrecasteaux islands of Papua New Guinea.

APPLEGARTH: AN AUSTRALIAN FAMILY ABROAD IN 1970

ISBN: 9780980282795
Paperback 404 pages
Includes photographs $39.95

Adventure with us as we sail to England. We make our home in 'Applegarth,' in Meopham, a village in Kent, but we travel in our motorized caravan at every opportunity, visit relatives and friends, spend summer on 'the continent' and immerse ourselves enthusiastically in history and tradition.

CHRISTIAN NOVEL

BALM OF BEERBURRUM

ISBN: 978098028272

6 Paperback 256 pages

$17.95

Violet Anderson lives in Kew, but her family home is in Monbulk. When her fiancé breaks their engagement she is so upset that she questions the existence of a loving God. Then her boss sends her on an assignment to Queensland's Sunshine Coast. Can she reconnect with God there and find balm for her wounded heart?

MISCELLANEOUS

CHRISTMAS CARD RECORD BOOK

ISBN: 9780980282740

Hard cover 136 pp. $19.95

This book gives a useful way to keep records of giving and receiving Christmas cards. Each letter of the alphabet has a page on preparation for the season and includes making plans, drawing up lists, creating decorations, making cards, Christmas recipes, hints on travel with children, holiday pet-care and games for Christmas Day.

B. J. SCOTT-BRANAGAN

Bronwen Scott-Branagan is a retired teacher who later turned author, a journey that she loves.

With over four decades of professional experience in education she has shown vision and dedication as a teacher, teacher-librarian ESL/EFL teacher, missionary and university lecturer. She has taught at all levels from preschool through primary and secondary levels in public schools in Australia and England, church schools in Australia and Papua New Guinea and as an Associate Professor at St. John's University in Taiwan.

She has degrees from a number of institutions, including Monash University, the University of Melbourne and William Carey International University, USA. Her qualifications include A.L.C.M, M.A.A.Sc., T.P.T.C., B.Ed. (School Librarianship), M.A. (Psycholinguistics and Theology), M.A. Hons. (Applied Linguistics), and D.Ed. (Applied Linguistics).

A number of her books are available from bookshops and may also be obtained directly from Dr. Scott-Branagan.

Phone: (613) 95979112 Email: bronwens@nex.net.au